Hale Irwin's Smart Golf

Hale Irwin's Smart Golf..................

WISDOM AND STRATEGIES FROM THE "THINKING MAN'S GOLFER"

..................Hale Irwin

WITH Robin McMillan and Jim Hartley

Quill

A HarperResource Book
An Imprint of HarperCollins*Publishers*

HarperCollins books may be purchased for educational, business, or sales promotional use. For information, please write to: Special Markets Department, HarperCollins Publishers, Inc., 10 East 53rd Street, New York, New York 10022.

Originally published in hardcover by HarperCollins in 1999 under the title *Smart Golf*.

First HarperResource paperback edition published in 2001.

Library of Congress Cataloging-in-Publication Data
Irwin, Hale.
    [Smart golf]
    Hale Irwin's smart golf : wisdom and strategies from the "thinking man's golfer" / Hale Irwin.
    p. cm. — (A HarperResource book)
Originally published as: Smart golf, 1999.
Includes index.
ISBN 0-06-272068-6
    1. Golf. 2. Golf—Psychological aspects. I. Title: Smart golf.
    II. Title. III. Series.
GV965.I77 2001
796.352'3—dc21

00-053904

01 02 03 04 05 ❖/RRD 10 9 8 7 6 5 4 3 2 1

Contents.........................

Introduction..................

Professional golf at its highest level is filled with smart golfers. Take a few of my peers. Jack Nicklaus is absolutely blessed with talent but that alone is not what separated him from the pack. What did was his concentration and intelligence when approaching how best to play a course. And whether a course called for an aggressive or a conservative style of play, he seldom deviated from what he had decided. Arnold Palmer? A much more aggressive player who knew he played better when he was aggressive, but not reckless. He knew the limits of his own game. Lee Trevino learned to get the most of his left-right trajectory—he's been smart enough to play the shot with which he is most comfortable.

You'll notice that these players are top professionals and, believe me, they did not get there through dumb luck and distance off the tee. They became immensely successful because—more than possessing good technique—they are all smart golfers.

What do we mean by "smart"? Well, first they know that low score wins. As obvious as that sounds, it's key to lowering your scores. How many times have you seen young players with powerful swings beaten by players twice their age who do not hit the ball as forcefully or as powerfully? It happens all the time because the youngsters get their kicks from looking good and hitting the ball long while the older, shorter hitters know that low score wins regardless of how it is achieved.

Smart players also know that low scores come from managing your game on and off the course. Smart *course* management covers everything you can do when on the golf course. It could be dropping down to a long-iron from the tee so you can keep the ball in the fairway. It could be using a middle-iron instead of a wedge when chipping around the green. It could mean laying up in front of a creek when it would take a career shot to clear it—even if you give up a stroke to par. And it could mean hitting a sand shot *away* from the hole rather than at it.

That, in fact, is what led to the first conversation I ever had with the coauthor of this book. In the third round of The Memorial Tournament in 1984, I hit my second shot on the 14th hole at Muirfield Village into a bunker back-left of the green. Now, Jack Nicklaus may be known for golf courses that are long and tough, but he also knows the value of a good short par four. At 363 yards, the 14th hole is reachable with a long-iron from the tee and an 8-iron from the fairway. But the green is long and narrow, and a creek cuts in front of it then winds along its right side. And, of course, the green slopes right down to the creek, which means that anything missing the green back-left is in real trouble. It's almost impossible to hold the green.

Here were my options: Hit a fluffy sand shot toward the hole and risk going into the water. If that happened I'd pick up a penalty stroke, drop within two clublengths of the margin of the hazard, no closer to the hole, hit my fifth shot from an uneven lie and then hope that I could one-putt for a double-bogey six.

Another option was to hit to a larger part of the green, back toward the hole, about 50 or 60 feet from the cup, and then get down in two putts for a bogey five (or make four with a little bit of luck). Were I to three-putt, I'd make double bogey. So it came down to this: even though I would be aiming away from the hole, there was a good chance I'd end up with a lower score. Option two won out, and bogey was indeed what went on the card.

A few days later, I received a call from an editor at *GOLF Magazine*. "I saw what happened on 14," he said. "A lot of people around me looked puzzled. They know you wear glasses, but figure that's so you *can* see where the hole is. Why on earth did you hit away from the hole?"

I went through the options, pointing out that hitting a miracle bunker shot had its merits, but the issue here was being able to write in as low a number as possible on the card. Or rather, one that was reasonable. A month or so later an item appeared in the magazine describing how I'd saved a stroke on that hole through some "smart" thinking. Hopefully some golfers learned something from that.

So that's an example of smart course management. But it's only one piece of the puzzle. There is also what's known as smart *game* management. This covers everything you can do to improve when not actually playing a round of golf. It includes practicing properly—with the emphasis on "properly"—making sure you're carrying the right equipment, staying fit, eating properly, and much more.

This is an area that probably is overlooked more than course management. Let's say you're playing a match in your club championship on a hot summer day. You're doing fine, all even, until on the 15th hole you feel your legs beginning to tire. You halve the hole. On the 16th hole you get into a little trouble, lose the hole, go one down, and now you have to win a hole to stay in the match. But your legs are really beginning to feel it, and when the legs go you have a tendency to use your arms more in the swing. Now your swing has changed. One down with two to play, and the swing that got you here is nowhere to be seen. Instead, you're lunging at the ball with your upper body, trying extra hard because if you can just give that extra effort then you'll win this hole and the next, and you'll be tired but happy. Well, now you're not thinking properly, either. Truth is, unless your opponent is in even worse physical shape, you have no chance.

Wouldn't it have made more sense if you had put in a few more miles on the exercise bicycle this summer? Was it really a good idea to eat a big plate of fried food for breakfast? Maybe a drink of water at the turn or on a few of the tees would have made a difference. Perhaps if you had paid attention to the shape your body was in before and during the round you could have closed out the match quite easily. And it wouldn't have taken much effort.

It's also smart not to play too much. I've long believed that if you play too much golf, you reach a point of diminishing returns. You may be physically and mentally worn out, you may not be thinking clearly. You certainly are not in the right shape to perform at your highest level.

During my first few years on Tour, I was a workhorse, playing between 32 and 36 events a year. I began to realize that I was performing poorly toward the end of the year. When I cut back my schedule to around 23 events, I started playing better year-round. I was mentally and physically relaxed, and was able to cut down on traveling and spend more time with my family. I was getting more out of the *quality* of my starts than the quantity of them.

Sadly, a lot of players do not think along these lines—and it is those players who will benefit most from this book. And not just high-handicappers. How often have you heard it said that it's easier to get from a 24 handicap to a 16 than it is to get from a four to a two? Believe me, there is not much technically different between most fours and most twos, but I'll bet anything that the twos play a little bit smarter. They settle for a bogey rather than try for the tough par that ends up a double. If they're about to play a course with small greens, they leave the 1-iron in the garage and add another wedge. They do not stand on the practice tee pounding balls; they practice the areas of their games that need the most practice. And they take care of themselves physically so they're mentally alert as well.

Let me put it this way. Every golfer, regardless of age, skill, or physique, has a brain—so every golfer should know how to use it.

To that end, *Hale Irwin's Smart Golf* differs from other golf books. It won't show you an ideal swing and then tell you that's how you should be swinging (although it will give a few pointers about swinging smartly). It instead will focus on getting the most out of the game you already have. And, as everything we discuss is firmly rooted in logic, a smarter game will be something you can hold on to, unlike so many swing changes golfers make. Band-aids, after all, eventually fall off.

I've learned the hard way that playing smart and getting the most out of my game is the only way to succeed. Put another way, there are a lot of ways to play golf—you just have to find the one that's right for you.

I could never hit the ball as long as Jack Nicklaus or Arnold Palmer or putt like Ben Crenshaw or, before him, Bobby Locke. But I soon realized that I didn't have to. Nicklaus, for example, may have been one of golf's longest hitters but his bread and butter was his ability to hit greens in regulation (two strokes on a par four, three on a par five). He was able to do that only because he was an accurate driver, and accuracy counts more than length. I figured that if I also could hit greens in regulation, then his advantage would be limited.

And Arnold? He was known as a great recovery artist, and he truly was—but he also was able to hit fairways regularly.

Here's a statistic that may shock you. In the 1990s, the era of the driver—who among us hasn't switched to an extra-long driver with oversized head?—only one U.S. Open champion has finished in the Top 35 in driving distance in the same year. Want to take a shot at our lone bopper? Big Ernie Els, Open winner in 1994 and '97? Sorry. Ernie was 52nd in driving distance in '97 and didn't play on the PGA Tour often enough in '94 to be measured. Payne Stewart in '91? Payne is a long hitter, but even he was 65th during the year in driving distance. The 1990 Open champion? No, because that would be me, and I finished 164th in driving distance, the lowest of any U.S. Open champion in the '90s (but I'll suffer that ignominy gladly in order to belong to such a select group of players).

No, the only Open champion this decade who also can be considered one of the longest drivers is Steve Jones, winner at Oakland Hills in 1996, and 10th on Tour that year with an average poke of 280 yards. Distance, you see, isn't everything.

Players win Open Championships because they play smart golf when it counts most—on tough courses in the heat of battle. I actually have a reputation for winning Opens on some of the toughest courses (although there isn't a single U.S. Open course that could be described as easy): Winged Foot, outside New York, in 1974; Inverness, in Toledo, in 1979; and Medinah, in Chicago in 1990. I also have a reputation for hitting good long irons, the 2-irons I hit to the final green at Winged Foot, to the 13th green in the final round at Inverness, and to the 16th green in the playoff with Mike Donald at Medinah, and that certainly helps when you're not the longest hitter in the field. But looking back, I'd have to say that smart course management made the difference.

Let's take a few examples:

In 1974 at Winged Foot, I took a two-stroke lead to the final hole; at least that was what I was told by a marshal. In those days there were far fewer scoreboards on the course. A safe play would have been to hit a 3-wood or a 1-iron, because I really didn't want to hit into the rough. But the 18th at Winged Foot doglegs to the left, and I knew I had to get around the corner in order to have a clear shot at the green. I suppose if I'd really smoked a 3-wood I may have reached the corner, but the wind was blowing from left to right, working against me. We'll touch on this in a few other places in this book, but let me emphasize this right now: It's always a good idea to play the hole backwards. I had to hit the green in two, and therefore had to reach the corner, and therefore had to hit driver. Some spectators may have been surprised to see me pull out the driver, figuring that I was bound to crash and burn, but in fact it was my only play.

So I hit a good drive, down the right-center of the fairway, and was left with 194 yards. I pulled out a 2-iron. That was more than enough to get there, but I was thinking backwards again. I wanted to be *above* the hole, not the usual thinking on U.S. Open greens. Usually, you want to leave yourself with an uphill putt. Not here. Although it may not look severe on television, the 18th green at Winged Foot sits high above the fairway. I could have hit 3-iron and been right on the margin, but I knew I had to avoid the area short and to the right. I figured it made more sense to fly the ball past the pin to where the target area was bigger. As it turned out, I hit a good shot to about 20 feet above the hole and, although I really wanted to make birdie, I two-putted for par and the victory.

That was a perfect example of how I was smart enough to focus on what I had to do in order to do what I *wanted* to do. But if you lose sight of what you want to do, and became overcome by the situation, then instead of you controlling the situation, it controls you. A good example of that is what happened to me in the 1979 Open at Inverness.

In that championship, I was three strokes clear of the field beginning my final round. I told myself that this was my tournament to win or lose, and decided to think as though I was tied for the lead. That was the position in which I'd begun on Thursday, and I'd played well enough, and thought well enough, to build up a good lead. If I could play the same kind of golf in the final round—going with a club if I felt comfortable with it, hitting to the fat of the greens—then it was going to take a heck of a score to beat me.

After nine holes, I'd extended my lead to six strokes. With two holes to play, my lead was five. At this point I told myself I'd won the tournament, and that was not a smart thing to do.

I let my guard down. I became less intense. I made mental mistakes. I also made a lazy swing on my tee shot, sort of guided the ball out there, and the ball ended up the right rough. After watching my 5-iron recovery come down in a greenside bunker, short and left, I thinned the bunker shot over the green. This was not going the way I'd planned. I was lying three and still wasn't on the green! I chipped on, past the hole, and two-putted for double bogey. I still had a three-stroke lead, but I was doing things I hadn't done through the first 70 holes. I wasn't playing smart.

On 18, when I should have played short off the tee— all week I'd hit 4-wood or 2-iron because the 18th hole at Inverness is only about 350 yards long—I let myself hit driver. Again I found the rough. Again I found a greenside bunker. This time I got the ball onto the green and two-putted for par and a two-stroke victory.

But it was poor that I played 70 holes of smart golf and then allowed myself to coast. It's like a sprinter going all out for 90 yards then coasting.

Then there are moments when you have to take chances. On the final hole of the 1998 U.S. Senior Open, for example, I played a shot I might not normally have played.

The 18th at Riviera Country Club in California is a tough, dogleg right that climbs to a small green set in an amphitheater of deep kikuyu rough. I'd started the tournament poorly, carding a 77 in the first round. Come Friday, however, I'd put that round behind me and settled on a game plan: Hit fairway, hit greens, and disregard hole locations. Forget about what I had done yesterday or what I might have to do tomorrow. Focus on what will work today. Commit to each shot and hit it. No, *really* commit.

It worked. By the time I got to 18, I was tied for the lead with Vicente Fernandez. I drove the ball in the fairway and, with the pin cut on a plateau in the back-left of the green, I now had two options.

Driving them was that kikuyu rough. If I were to go for the hole, I would risk catching the rough to the left or to the back of the green, and once in there I might never get out. The worst score I wanted to make was par, and the chances of making par from the rough are slim. The other option was to hit to the front-right of the green, the safe part, and either make a miracle birdie putt or make two putts for par.

The second option was definitely the smart play—if I wanted to go into a playoff. But I've hoed that row, and felt that this was time to be bold. I had come from a long way back, and something told me that this was no time to back off. Rather than hit a nice, safe 5-iron, I decided to take a little off a 4-iron and go right at the flag.

The shot landed inches from the left rough and came to a halt about 12 feet beyond and to the left of the hole. The putt was dead straight, and I drained it to win what at that point in my career was my most sought-after title.

Hopefully such a dramatic ending will quiet those critics who suggest that the senior circuit isn't competitive. It's true that the courses we play may be set up a little easier than the layouts on the regular tour, and it's true our games may not be as sharp as they once were. But competitiveness is a personality thing and competitive people don't become pushovers the day they turn 50. Guys like Trevino, Larry Nelson, Raymond Floyd, Gil Morgan, and soon Tom Watson, Lanny Wadkins, Tom Kite—how can anyone say they're not competitive? They come from a generation that didn't blast balls from the tee using ultra-long drivers with mammoth heads, or hit shots with irons designed to forgive. We learned to win by outsmarting the other guy, and that still goes on the Senior Tour. Let the regular tour hit it 300 and stick it stiff with the power-wedge play. We're just trying to get an edge any way that we can.

And the best way to do that is to be as smart as you can.

PART ONE ....

...........................Smart Game
                    Management

1

Getting Off to a Smart Start..................

SETTING OUT

One of the smartest things I did on joining the PGA Tour in the summer of 1968 was to jot down some goals. Given that this was the start of a whole new career, it was important to be clear about what I wanted to achieve and felt I *could* realistically achieve.

The first goal that appeared on the list was to play on weekends, which is another way of saying "make cuts." Winning a tournament was important, of course—that was another goal—but, with very few exceptions, no one has ever won a PGA Tour event, at least in the modern era, without first making the cut. It's not unlike playing a golf hole. In order to achieve one thing, you first have to achieve something else. To give yourself a good chance of par or even birdie, for example, you want to hit the green with your approach, and to give yourself a good chance of *that* you have to hit a good drive. First things first.

A related goal was to make a *lot* of cuts, because that way you learn to feel the pressure of contention. The idea is to strengthen everything about your game—swing, mental process, nerves—so when the clutch arrives you don't collapse. That comes only with a lot of experience.

And, finally, I wanted to make a few bucks. This was the *professional* tour, after all, and a tour pro who doesn't list making money as one of his goals is wasting his time.

You'll notice that "win a *major* championship" (as opposed to a regular Tour event) wasn't a goal, despite the fact that I went on to win three U.S. Open Championships. Why? Because it was important to be realistic, and what was very, *very* real in 1968 was Jack Nicklaus and Lee Trevino and Arnold Palmer and Billy Casper and Gary Player and Tom Weiskopf, and a bunch of other great players. My time would come.

So what happened? Well, after turning pro in the spring of 1968 and winning my tour card at Qualifying School that summer, I made the cut in the first tournament I played, the Memphis Open. I didn't make any money, however, because in those days you had to finish in the top 50 to cash in and I just missed out. Next up was the Canadian Open; I made that one, but again finished out of the money. But, beginning with the Cleveland Open the following week, I made the cut in each of my next 10 events. That was worth a shade more than $9,000 in prize money—as noted, it wasn't enough to make the cut to make money—good for 129th on the money list. That's not great, but making cuts helps you improve, and that translates into bigger checks. Ask anyone who plays or has played on the PGA Tour and they'll tell you that the quickest way to feel your confidence drain is to have to leave town Friday evening when many of your peers are still in the money with two rounds to play. It was something solid to build on. It was a good year.

Once you have achieved your goals, the smart thing to do is to make a new list. Now making cuts wasn't enough. My goals now included top-ten finishes, top-five finishes, and victories. I also split my goals into two lists: short-term and long-term. A year was short-term, five years was long. Nineteen sixty-nine saw my first top 10, the following year my first runner-up, the year after that my first victory. And in 1974, one year beyond my five-year plan, I won the U.S. Open.

So you can see, making new goals as you progress is as important as setting realistic goals to begin with—and not only in golf. Take a football coach who inherits a 1–15 team. His first goal is to surround himself with the personnel—players, mainly, but also back-office staff—that can give him a winning record. If he can swing a deal or two he might think of making the playoffs. If he can do that, then next year he's definitely thinking of playoffs, and a few good signings could put the Super Bowl on his list. Once you're there, then, as Lee Trevino once put it, "It's just, baby, how *bad* do you want it?"

Or take the business world. The head of a major company that's been down on its luck first wants to get it in the black. Then he (or she) wants to make a profit. Next he will want to increase the profit margin and become number one in the field. And, meanwhile, the ultimate goal will be to get the share price up to reward those who invested in the company in the first place. It's all about setting realistic goals and reaching them, and then moving on from there.

SETTING GOALS FOR YOURSELF

How do you set golf goals for yourself? Well, first you must make a very real assessment of your abilities, because before you can get anywhere, you must know where you're starting from. Joining the tour, I thought of myself as a tough competitor who didn't make many mistakes. That was the foundation.

And your own foundation? It depends. You could be a complete beginner, who has to work on every aspect of his game. You could be an experienced player who wins some tournaments but can't win the big one. You could be a player who hits the ball a long way but also hits it a long way off target. If you can honestly determine where your problems lie, then you will know what sort of goals to set.

Because it's the aim of every golfer, no matter his or her style, to score better, whether during a casual round or a local major championship, it really doesn't matter what sort of player you are; it's just important that you know. Talk with friends, your club pro, or people you've played with to help you find out. Once you've settled on who you are, you can start mapping out your goals.

Setting goals forces you to stop and think about your game: your strengths, weaknesses, what you want to achieve—even your level of commitment to improving. Setting goals is a road map to improvement. As long as the goals are realistic, you can track your improvement. If you're on track, you can set new goals for further improvement. If you're behind schedule, you can review your goals and make necessary adjustments.

Goals come in many forms. There are technique goals (I want to improve the swing on my tee shots) and scoring goals (I want to play 18 holes without a double bogey). There are what I'll call winning goals (I want to win the club championship), and handicap goals (I want to get down to a single digit). There are round-by-round goals (I want to work on long-iron play during this round).

You should choose these goals, and others, based on how you play right now and how much work you're willing to invest in improving. They all are important goals. But, broadly speaking, the truly crucial goals—those that apply to every golfer on earth—are *timing* goals.

In other words, you should have long-term goals, mid-term goals, and short-term goals.

Although these are flexible goals, you should first fix on a long-term goal. Again, it's up to your own judgment. You may be playing, say, to a 13 handicap, and want to get down to six or seven within five years. But it doesn't make a lot of sense to set that as a goal if you're about to take on a new job that will require an immense amount of traveling.

Once you've fixed your long-term goal—five or six years—work out a mid-term goal, for the next two or three years. Your short-term goal should cover only the upcoming year.

Now things get interesting. What it takes for you to meet your short-term goal will determine whether you should change your mid-term goal and, of course, your long-term goal. It's the golf-hole analogy again. In order to meet a long-term goal (get the ball in the hole), we have to have a mid-term goal (get the ball on the green), and a short-term goal (hit the ball safely off the tee). If working backwards is planning a hole and working forward is playing it, then setting long-, mid-, and short-term goals is planning your success, and executing short-, mid-, and long-term goals is achieving it.

TRACKING YOUR IMPROVEMENT

Once you have mapped out your goals, you will have to devise a way of tracking your performance. It's not enough to say "Hey, I used to shoot 82–84 most days, now I'm shooting 78–80; I must be getting better." It is key that you know *why* you're scoring better, not only so that you can continue to score better but because at some point you'll want to shoot even lower. To get to the second stage, in other words, you must know and understand how you got to the first.

Tracking your game is not difficult, mainly because a round of golf can be easily broken down statistically. As you continue to break down your rounds, patterns will begin to emerge, and you will be able to spot your weaknesses and strengths. You then can take the appropriate action to improve.

Having said that, it's also not a bad idea to use a statistical report to help establish your goals. Pro-ams are full of golfers who miss a ton of fairways and are generally poor off the tee, yet they may boom one or two big ones out there and walk off thinking they're actually good drivers! Were they to keep numbers on their games, in this instance on driving accuracy, they would see that driving needs the most work.

We keep ten statistical categories on the Senior PGA Tour (at least for public consumption; the Tour's computers can spit out just about anything we need). The same goes for the PGA Tour. These are:

1. Scoring average

2. Driving distance (measured on two holes at each tournament, then averaged out)

3. Driving accuracy (amount of fairways hit from the tee)

4. Total driving (combination of distance and accuracy)

5. Greens in regulation ("regulation" is one stroke on a par three, two on a par four, and three on a par five)

6. Putting leaders (average putts taken in greens hit in regulation)

7. Sand saves (percentage of ups-and-downs for par)

8. Birdie leaders (average birdies per round)

9. Eagle leaders (average holes played between each eagle)

10. All-around (total standings in all categories)

Those are the basics, and they work for most touring pros. What aren't publicized, but are pretty useful, are round-by-round averages—a player's average for each first, second, and third round (the regular Tour also has fourth rounds, but the Senior PGA Tour doesn't play many four-round tournaments). If, for example, my third-round average was noticeably higher than that of my main competitors, it would make sense to break down each third round to find some pattern. Too many bogeys on the opening holes, perhaps. Maybe just too many pars from start to finish.

The statistics have improved on both tours in recent years. It used to be that both birdies and eagles were rated as totals—who had the most, in other words—and that contributed to what is termed "all-around" standings. Problem was, some guys rode roller coasters at each event, matching each birdie and eagle with double and triple bogeys! Yet they still were considered to have good all-around games!

And for many years on the PGA Tour, putts were counted as totals. The result was that such great players as Greg Norman and Tom Kite were never thought of as good putters whereas lesser-known players were. Why was this? Because if a Tour pro hits a green in regulation, more often than not he'll take two putts for par. But if he misses the green, he'll chip on and scramble for par. The two scores are the same, but one takes fewer putts. In other words, putting expressed as a total was a better indicator of bad iron play than good putting. It made no sense.

Fortunately, the Tour has changed course so that putting is measured as an average of putts taken in greens hit in regulation (GIR). It rates those who can get the little white thing in the cup *once they're on the dance floor*. It doesn't measure how long the first putt may be, but it's not a bad gauge of a good putter. Put it this way, a player who finishes well in the GIR category and poorly in putting really should spend more time on the practice green.

With the exception of the all-around category and possibly measuring birdies and eagles, the above categories work for the amateur golfer. But I'd add a few:

- Par threes in regulation. Pros pick up strokes at par fives; amateurs can do best at par threes, where they face an approach with a flat lie, and a ball on a tee. Doubles on par threes will kill you.

- Average putts per hole. Yes, in addition to greens in regulation.

- Average putts taken after chips. Getting up-and-down successfully means one. That's what you want to work toward.

- Chip saves. Very similar to the above.

- Putts made per round by distance. Up to four feet, four to eight feet, and so on.

- Putts missed per round by distance.

- Three putts per round.

- Penalty strokes per round. Make sure you consider *how* you got them.

- Number of times approach shots come up short. Fuzzy Zoeller used to say that when an amateur was, say, stuck between a soft seven and a hard eight, he'd tell him to take the seven and hit it as hard as he could. He's right. Most amateurs think they can reach with too little club.

- Recovery shots per round (an indicator of how often you found trouble) and percentage of successful recoveries.

- Breakdown of scoring into birdies, pars, bogeys, double bogeys, and worse.

- Mental errors per round. You'll have to be really honest on this one, but it's worth it.

HOW TO TRACK EACH ROUND

Rule number one. Don't do it after each hole if you'd be holding up the group behind. It is a good idea to jot things down when they're fresh in your memory, but you should do so only if there's time at the next tee. If not, do it immediately after your round or—if you plan on enjoying a post-round snifter with playing companions who probably don't care a lick about charting your score—as soon as you get home. Just don't wait until the details fade.

If the scorecard of the course you're playing has a course map or individual hole diagrams, mark where each shot ended up, and what club you hit. Somewhere on the card you also should note the time you played, the course conditions and the weather conditions. After all an 85 shot in perfect conditions is a lot worse than an 85 shot in rain and a howling gale.

You then should fill out a chart—you can make it yourself—with all the statistical categories listed above. It shouldn't take too many rounds for you to start seeing patterns. However, don't rush out to the practice green immediately if you see a few too many three-putts. Track your numbers a little longer before jumping to conclusions.

There also are services that will track your stats for you. Most advertise in the classified sections of the major golf publications. You might also want to seek them out through some of the golf web sites. In such cases, you'll be provided with a "kit" to track various aspects of your game. The stat service then crunches the numbers and offers you advice.

A SMART GOLF ACTION PLAN

Once you set your long- and mid-term goals, it's time to get moving with your short-term goals. But first split the task into two areas:

1. **Managing Yourself.** This is about managing how you improve and not about hitting balls (except in practice). It should include getting the right equipment, starting a fitness regime, getting advice on the proper diet, mapping out a practice schedule, settling on a teacher and taking lessons, and deciding which tournaments, if any, you may want to enter.

2. **Managing Your Game.** It should include everything from developing a pre-shot routine to learning how

to save strokes around the green. It also should include learning more about the physical and mental aspects of golf.

Do you recall that "win a major championship" was not one of my goals when I joined the PGA Tour?

I lied.

Sort of.

I didn't just write down the goals and stash them away somewhere. They were a work in progress. I first listed everything I wanted to achieve, then scratched off stuff that was really unrealistic, then put a few things back. It took a good two weeks to come up with a list— and winning a major championship was on and off that list more often than anything.

After a few years on Tour, "win the U.S. Open" made it onto the list of goals. Goals get updated as you progress, remember? And in 1974, at Winged Foot, the dream came true.

But "win three U.S. Opens" never was a goal. Only four players have won more than three U.S. Opens: Nicklaus, Ben Hogan, Bobby Jones and, back at the turn of the century, Willie Anderson. I'm the only other golfer who has won more than two. So, how could it have been legitimate to make three U.S. Opens a goal when starting out?

When I won the first, it felt so good, so invigorating, that I thought immediately of winning another. And when that came along five years later, at Inverness, you bet number three became a goal.

Interestingly, when the third did arrive, it proved to be

a good example of how you should set goals and adjust them along the way.

I qualified for the 1990 U.S. Open at Medinah only with a special exemption based on my two previous victories (the 10-year exemption for winning in 1979 had expired the year before). That the United States Golf Association had extended me an invitation determined my first goal. Rather than show up, play a couple of "ceremonial rounds," miss the cut by a stroke or two, and go home satisfied that no one really expected me to do any better, I decided to play well enough so that neither the USGA nor I would be embarrassed.

Winning wasn't too realistic a goal, but the top-15 scores and ties earn automatic berths for the following year's Open. Earning an invite back seemed like a good way of showing my appreciation, so that became my second goal.

I opened with rounds of 69–70, which not only made the cut but gave me sole possession of fifth place. In the third round a 74 dropped me to 21st—disappointing, but I still was in the hunt. The top 15 remained my goal as the final day dawned.

I was even par through 10 holes, which lifted me into 16th place. I figured getting back to the clubhouse one stroke under par wouldn't lose me any ground and probably would lift me up the board a bit. That was my next goal.

A birdie at 11 got me to one under and into the top 10. I remember telling myself, "Just relax. Let's see where we might go from here."

I birdied 12. Into the top 10. Birdied 13. Top seven.

Birdied 14. Top four! Now *this* was the situation: I was a two-time Open champion and had been in contention a couple of other times, so the pressure wasn't new. There was no crushing gallery of fans (even though I was playing with Greg Norman). Curtis Strange was in the hunt for his third consecutive Open that year, and the 54-hole leaders had teed off two hours after our group. They were the players the fans and the television cameras were focusing on. For the first time all day—all year!—winning the U.S. Open became my goal.

I parred 15 through 17. At seven under, I was two strokes off the lead held by Mike Donald—but he had an awful lot of U.S. Open golf left to play. On the tee of the par-four 18th, I told myself that a birdie to go to eight under might not win the Open, but there was a *very* good chance it would tie for the lead. The immediate goal, then, was to make a three.

It wasn't easy. After hitting a so-so 7-iron to the front of the green, I faced a 45-foot putt with a good seven feet of right-to-left break and a large hump directly between me and the hole. It was impossible.

You know what happened next. The putt rolled up and down and round and flew into the cup. I couldn't believe it. It seemed like all the adrenaline that comes with the drama and excitement of a 23-year career in professional golf was now coursing through my veins. I jumped up, pumped my fists in the air, and high-fived everyone I could reach. People couldn't believe what they were seeing. I had never been known for outward signs of emotion, but here I was running around like a kid, celebrating with the fans.

The next day, of course, I beat Donald in sudden death after tying him through 18 holes. From out of the blue, I had my third U.S. Open, and an invite for the next 10 years. And a lot had to do with the fact that from day one I had crystal-clear goals and calmly evaluated and adjusted them as the situation changed and the circumstances dictated.

Now let's show you how to do that with your own golf game.

2

The Tools of the Trade ....

Life used to be so simple. Three networks, three car manufacturers, and no lite, dry, or ice beers. In golf, woods were made of wood and irons were made out of steel. The heads on the woods were made from solid persimmon, or occasionally laminated from various layers of wood pressed and sealed together. Irons were forged, which is to say hammered out of a solid block of hot metal. Most of the weight was concentrated in the sole of the club to help get the ball airborne. If you understood these things, then finding the right equipment was as simple as finding the right carton of milk in the dairy aisle. Of course milk got complicated, too.

What happened in golf was that the game took off like a rocket. From the late 1970s through the mid-1990s, millions of new players flocked to golf. Equipment companies, which already were running a pretty good business, realized that they were not only able to market to this massive new audience, but that this was a group that was happy to be marketed to. Tell us about clubs that hit the ball longer, golfers said. Give us new materials. Give us new technology. Give us new designs.

Why this was the case in an age when we regularly complain about marketing being too aggressive is simple. When people get passionate about something, they can't get enough "stuff." If you have any doubts about this, take a look at any ardent fishermen (and there aren't many other kinds). They usually have huge collections of rods and reels. They buy books. They try different lures, different baits. They'll subscribe to magazines that tell them how to fish better and where to catch bigger fish. They'll pore through catalogs, sometimes without any real intention of buying anything. They just want to keep up with the stuff.

Golfers are the same, and that's because golf, like fishing, is primarily a *participant* sport. It's true that the pro tours have never been healthier, that television networks are spending massive amounts of money on golf, but if you figure that on any given weekend a little over 200 top touring professionals are playing in a tour event on the weekend, and that there are tens of millions of amateurs playing at exactly the same time, then the game really is about amateur participation.

The result? Manufacturers scramble to find different routes to the same place—a purchase. Golfers face a myriad of choices when purchasing new equipment. And all the companies claim essentially the same things—their clubs hit the ball longer and straighter with less chance of mishits, their balls fly longer (although you don't hear much about accuracy)—but they make their claims in different ways. As noted, golfers like this. It's a very healthy relationship.

You could be forgiven for assuming that, with so much new equipment out there, you should be able to close your eyes, pick up anything, and buy yourself a better game. Well, yes, you probably would come up with something serviceable, equipment that will get you around the course without any injury.

But that wouldn't be too smart. Remember our concept of smart game management: doing everything possible to improve when not on the course. The idea is not just to buy equipment that will help you play, but equipment that will help you *improve*.

So what should you buy? Well, I would never say that there is a specific club that works best, because what works depends on the type of golfer you are and where you play. The smart thing, therefore, is to learn the various characteristics of golf equipment, and then figure out—with a little help from the experts—what works best for you.

CLUB CHARACTERISTICS

The basics elements of golfclub design are clubhead weight and its distribution, loft, lie, shaft length, feel (technically it's known as swingweight), overall weight, shaft flex, grip size and type. Let's take them one by one.

Clubhead Weight and Distribution

The two main types of clubhead distribute weight in radically different ways. In forged clubs, sometimes known as blades, the weight is concentrated along the soles of the clubhead. This helps impart backspin on the ball which, combined with the aerodynamic effect of the ball's dimples, makes the ball rise. These are difficult clubs to hit. Or, rather, they are so unforgiving that only the best ball strikers should use them. On the other hand, they provide more "feel" for players who can strike the ball consistently with the sweetspot of the clubface.

Because of this, the vast majority of pros used to play with blades, but with advances in equipment manufacturing techniques and new materials, the other type of club-

---

My First Sets of Clubs

My dad got me into golf when I was six or seven. He was a good athlete, about a 10-handicap. He gave me some cut-down clubs held together with electrical tape. I got my first half-set when I was 12—I don't remember the make—and got my first full set a few years later. Sam Snead Blue Ridge woods and irons. I was so proud of them I must have polished the chrome off them.

We lived in a small town in the southeast of Kansas, close to Joplin, Mo. called Baxter Springs. We had a nine-hole public course with sand greens. In fact, when we moved to Boulder, Co., when I was 14, I had played on grass greens only three times, twice in Joplin and once while on vacation in Boulder.

In my teenage years, Wilson Staff Haig Ultra were the clubs to own in my peer group. As a pro, I stuck with Wilson for 25 years, and for a long time I hit Cleveland Classic woods. It's only a few years ago that I switched to Cobra.

head—investment-cast—has become very popular on all the main tours. While blades are made by hammering a solid piece of molten metal into shape, investment-cast clubs are made by pouring hot metal into a mold. The aim here is to distribute the weight around the outside of the clubface; it's called perimeter weighting. The idea is that if the weight is distributed evenly, or close to evenly, around the perimeter of the clubface, then shots hit on the clubface but away from the sweetspot (on the toe or heel, for example) still will fly a good distance because there is weight behind the area that has struck the ball.

The same principle applies to woods. Metal woods are perimeter weighted; wooden woods are not. But even the best players hit metal woods for one simple reason: While you want to hit accurate tee shots, this area of the game does not have to be as accurate as iron play, relatively speaking, and the feedback from feel is not so crucial. (Don't get me wrong, though, accuracy is still your most important asset when on the tee.)

On an average course your target from the tee is a fairway 40 yards wide (27–29 yards in the U.S. Open), but a shot hit to a green must hit a target up to 10 yards wide. Even the top players are prepared to give up feel for the extra yards that will mean they can be even more accurate on their approach shots. That's why you'll have to hunt far and wide just to find a wood made out of, yes, wood.

Loft

I could run down the loft for various irons (and woods) but it's not really important for you to know them. It's more important that lofts be consistent from club to club, and it's most important that you know the distances you hit each club.

One reason that I'm reluctant to relate the different lofts for different clubs is that, while certain industry standards do exist, a lot of manufacturers have been claiming more distance from their clubs simply by delofting them. "Our 5-iron now hits 10 yards longer," a manufacturer might say, but that's mainly because it now has the loft of a 4-iron.

The interesting aspect of this is what it has done to the high-loft area of equipment. If your 9-iron is now an 8-iron and your pitching wedge is now a 9-iron, what replaces the pitching wedge? The sand wedge? No, because its primary function is to escape from sand, so delofting the club defeats that purpose. Instead, the pitching wedge is increasingly being replaced by what is called a gap wedge: It fills the gap that once was occupied by the pitching wedge.

Lie

This often is overlooked, probably because it's such a "small" area. When golfers pick up a club, they may waggle it and take a close look at the clubhead, but they seldom check out the lie angle.

To explain: The lie of a club is the angle between the sole of the club and the shaft of the club when you address the ball. If the toe is too far off the ground, then the lie is too "upright." You should have a smaller angle between the head and the shaft—a flatter lie. But if the heel is at all off the ground at address, then the lie is too flat. You should have more upright lies.

Note I referred to the toe being "too far" off the ground. This is because, when your lies are perfect, the toe should be very slightly off the ground at address, perhaps by one or two degrees. This is because the natural motion of the golf swing forces the toe to "dip," so that as the clubface strikes the ball, the sole of the club is level with the ground. Remember: A little off the ground at address will be flat at impact.

Why is this so important? Simply because if the lie isn't correct, then all the technology that has gone into the design (not to mention the money you spent on the clubs) will be wasted because there is either a space below the toe or below the heel at impact. A club that is too flat at impact will hit the ball to the right. A club that is too upright will hit the ball to the left. Furthermore, on shots where you take a divot—and there are few shots when you will *not* take some size of divot—then the club will not dig into the ground evenly as it makes contact with the ball. With one end of the clubhead digging in first, the club will twist at impact, and it will be difficult to hit a good shot.

I emphasize the importance of correct lies for two reasons. One I just covered: You will not have good, clean impact without proper lies. And two: It's a very simple thing to check. All you have to do is take your normal stance! If your lies are off, it's very simple to adjust them. It may seem like a minor detail in the purchase of the proper equipment, but smart golfers take care of the minor details, too.

Shaft Length

In a nutshell, the shorter the length of the shaft, the easier the club is to control, and the more accurate your shots should be. This applies to just about any situation. The only exception you're likely to run into with any sort of frequency is the lie with the ball below your feet. If the shot can be played with a club of less loft, then the extra length of the shaft will be an advantage, but it's not a very smart idea to let the length of the shaft dictate the shot for you.

Shaft length is a huge issue with the driver. One of the key recent developments in the driver has been to take weight out of the hosel area (where the shaft connects to the clubhead), redistribute it to the head, and make the head out of a light clubhead material such as titanium. There's not necessarily a lot of heft to this combination, so manufacturers juice things up by increasing shaft length, and they are able to do this without increasing the overall weight of the club by using lighter materials. It really is a whole new ball game.

Basically, the longer the shaft, the greater the arc of your swing, and the greater the swing speed you should be able to produce. You can read of the many differences between the game of a touring professional and that of a good amateur; almost always mentioned is the short game, and sometimes length off the tee, but rarely is swing speed mentioned. Here are two absolute facts about pros: Their swing speed is far greater (125 mph versus 95 mph for an amateur, on average), and they control that speed consistently so the speed always is transferred efficiently and powerfully into the ball.

What good does it do to tell you this? Two reasons.

One is that swing speed is something you should think about working on. But, more important, just as it is easier to control clubs with short shaft lengths, so is it more difficult to control those that are longer. Few of today's drivers are *not* extra-long, which is to say 45 inches against the industry standard that was 43.5 or 44 a decade ago (when I started on Tour, the standard was 43 inches). It is just too easy to be seduced by the extra swing speed and, therefore, extra distance because the shaft of your driver is longer.

Be careful. Before you move to a driver whose shaft is longer than you've been used to, the smart thing is to take it out on the range and practice with it more than any other club. The last thing you want to do is put yourself behind the 8-ball off the tee.

And one other thing: Because smart players pay attention to the minor details, I suggested you check your lofts to make sure they are consistent, and your lies to make sure they are correct. Check your shaft lengths, too. Consistency from club to club (driver excepted) helps make the other checks worthwhile.

Feel

This is known technically as swingweight, and although there are countless clubmakers and experts on equipment who will protest that swingweight is a tangible measure and feel is just what a club feels like, I'd suggest the following difference: Most golfers don't understand swingweight; almost all golfers understand feel.

Swingweight is essentially the relationship between

the length of the shaft, the flex of the shaft, and the weight of the clubhead. If you change any or all of these properties, the swingweight will change. At this point, we should switch to feel because the heavier the swingweight, the more you'll feel the clubhead.

Feel is a big part of a smart golf game. If you like swinging clubs that give you better feel, it's probably because they're giving you feedback. A lot of players prefer this. They can feel mishits—off the heel, off the toe—and they can work out their problems.

There also is a school of thought that says graphite clubs and perimeter-weighted, investment-cast heads reduce feel around the green. I can't say I subscribe to that, but I can say that the golfers who say this understand that the short game is the area of golf that demands the most feel.

The Benefits of a 1-Iron

Much is made of whether an amateur golfer should carry a 1-iron. The prevalent thinking is that it's the toughest club to hit, and therefore you're not going to hit it very well, so why take it with you at all?

I understand that thinking, but I also know that:

1. My own ability to hit long irons has come in very useful on long, tight, tough courses—both from the fairway and from the tee.

2. The idea here is to improve by being smart. That doesn't mean that you automatically are smarter by carrying a 1-iron because it's part of a master plan. No, you should instead make being able to hit a 1-iron one of your goals, and then work toward it with a lot of practice on the range.

Overall Weight

The weight of the clubs you choose depends on what type of golfer you are. Some golfers like heavy clubs (and some are even strong enough to merit them). At the other end of the spectrum, there was the lightweight craze of the mid-1980s, when many pros switched to lighter clubs and watched their increased swingspeed create longer shots—then watched as their bodies adapted naturally, their swing speed slowed, and they were back to square one. The smart thing to do is find the weight of clubs that suits you and, if you must, err on the side of too light. There will be occasions when you're tired, and the extra weight will literally be a burden. One could make the argument that heavier clubs will increase swing speed (not true) and that heavier clubs will bulldoze your ball out of heavy rough. Perhaps, but it's smarter to have a club that you can control, because if you can't control your clubs easily, you won't have much control over your score.

Shaft Flex

I cannot attach enough importance to playing with the proper shafts. It doesn't matter how well you swing, how well you think, how well you behave away from the course—if you have the wrong shafts for your game, then you will not improve. It's like having a car with a great engine but lousy tires.

The more flex, the more "whip" in your shaft as you swing. Whip isn't always a good thing, and lack of whip doesn't help either. As a rule, with average swing speeds—for average amateurs—an extra flexible shaft will hook the ball, and a stiffer shaft will push the ball. By the same token, if you tend to hook the ball (probably because you swing too fast), you may want to think about a stiffer shaft, and if you tend to slice, you may want to look at more flex. Generally, speaking, most amateurs play with a shaft that's a little too stiff for them. You may want to experiment.

Kick Point

This describes the point on the shaft that bends the most during the swing. If the kick point is low on the shaft, the club sort of drop-kicks the ball, causing it to fly higher. A high kick-point, up near the grip, will make the ball fly lower.

Grip Size

Although most golfers can use standard grip sizes, it's worth the effort to test to make sure that you do indeed have the correct grip size. To do this, hold a club in your left hand, as you would if you were addressing a ball. The tips of your middle and fourth fingers should touch, very lightly, the pad of your thumb at its base.

If your fingers do not reach the pad, then your grips are too large, which can lead to a tendency to leave the club open at impact. And that results in either a push or slice. If your fingers overlap the pad, then your grips are too small, and the opposite could occur.

The only reason I know for employing the wrong grip size would be if you are having trouble with your sand game. Put an oversized grip on your sand wedge and you'll find it easier to keep the club open and moving through the sand. It might cause problems when you use your sand wedge from other parts of the course, however.

Grip Type

Rubber is the standard for most amateurs, while some pros prefer leather. If you feel you don't get a good enough grip on your clubs, consider switching to half-cord. These are grips with fabric woven into the underside. (Full cord has the fabric woven into the rubber on both sides of the grip.) They do allow for a firm grip but they also can be hard on your hands.

The big issue with grips really is how often you should change them, and I suppose that depends on how often you play. I change my grips every two or three months, except for the driver grip. I change that one every two weeks. Changing grips should be a matter of routine and not a matter of waiting until they feel too smooth, or until they show signs of "shine." That's like knowing a storm is approaching but waiting to see lightning before taking shelter. It's too late.

PUTTING IT ALL TOGETHER

It's one thing to know all the elements of golf club design. It's another thing to know what you need. I'd break the process down into three steps.

1. Determine your ball flight and pattern.

2. Seek advice.

3. Test-drive before you buy.

Determine Your Ball Flight and Pattern

You can do this on the course, but I'd advise some serious time on the range. You encounter too many sloping lies on a golf course, and you really have to hit from the same level lie over and over to see any patterns emerge. You also should try to hit straight shots; there's no point in concluding that you fade the ball, for example, if you're deliberately trying to hit fades!

And hit with several clubs. Driver, long iron, middle iron, short iron. Don't hit to targets; just concentrate on making clean contact and getting the ball to fly straight. You might even want to get another player to take a look at your game.

Finally, conduct these tests in windless conditions. If your ball keeps flying left, and there's a right-to-left crosswind, you'll learn more about the strength of the wind than about the natural aspects of your game.

Seek Advice

When you have concluded that you have a particular ball flight, seek help. If you belong to a club, go to the pro. Tell him or her what you've found. A good pro will take you back out to the range to confirm or adjust your determinations. And a *really* good pro will have swing analyzer equipment.

If you don't belong to a club, go to a driving range or even a retail golf store. You'd be surprised by how many pros at these places are fully certified by the PGA of America, the club pros' own organization.

Some equipment companies offer clubfitting services. They take various measurements (height, body shape, arm and leg measurements, etc.) and find what should be right for you. When clubfitting started in the 1970s and '80s, it was kind of a fad, a marketing trick by club companies to get more business. But as new materials and designs have emerged, clubfitting has become important, and the business has become so competitive that what these companies do can be very worthwhile.

Test-Drive Before You Buy

I cannot emphasize how important this is, for not only must you be able to hit the shots you want with new equipment, but you must also be comfortable with your clubs. Let's say, for example, that you have state-of-the-art clubs with low-torque shafts, oversized heads, a low kick-point, and perfect grips. The fact is that if you do not feel comfortable with these clubs, or if you find them unsightly, then you are not going to hit as many good shots. It sounds silly, but you should enjoy your clubs; enjoy taking them out of the bag, enjoy waggling them, and enjoy hitting balls with them. All the high technology that has gone into club design will mean nothing if you do not feel comfortable with your clubs.

CLUB MAKEUP

The United States Golf Association limits you to 14 clubs, and most players don't even need that many. I say you should have at least 20 (but only carry 14 at a time, of course). You should have driver, 3-wood, 4-wood, 5-wood, another utility wood (25–29 degrees of loft, with a ribbed sole), 1-iron through pitching wedge, a gap wedge, a sand wedge, and a lob wedge, a light putter and a heavy putter. You should choose the 14 clubs that give you maximum scoring possibilities.

Having said that, I must confess that I don't change my equipment much to suit different courses. I seldom carry a third wedge, for example. I will, however, replace my 4-wood with a 1-iron if I'm playing a course with long par threes, or if I expect the conditions to be windy, such as at the British Open. The 1-iron in the latter case allows me to play lower shots that will benefit from the roll of links courses. On the Senior Tour, there's not a lot of call for a 1-iron.

I also believe it's smart for you to determine whether changing your club makeup will advance your cause or hurt it. If you conclude that it may hurt it, abandon the idea of changing club makeups, and work on getting the most out of one set.

Here are some things to consider:

- If you do plan to put a different club in your bag, make certain you have practiced with it until you are sure about which situations it works best in and what it does to the ball. You cannot pull it out of your bag and ask yourself, "Now what does this club do?"

- Ignore those who tell you to use a light putter on fast greens and a heavier putter on slow greens.

- A utility wood is a viable option. There is nary a golf course out there that doesn't have some spot that requires an escape shot. More and more utility woods are also seeing a lot of action from the fairway, when shots of 200-plus yards are called for.

- A lob wedge can be useful on a course with small, well-guarded greens.

- A 5-wood is a good replacement for the 1- and 2-irons if you're having trouble hitting them.

- If you're having trouble off the tee, take the driver but pack the 3-wood, too. Here's another good tip: Try a lady's driver. It usually has the loft of a 2-wood and maybe a more manageable shaft length. You may have to enlarge the grip to fit your hands, however.

- If you're a senior, consider replacing long- and middle-iron with metal woods. They make fuller contact, especially on tough lies in short rough.

THE MOST IMPORTANT CLUB IN YOUR BAG

It's true you have a better chance of scoring well if you hit more fairways from the tee, and therefore the drive may be the most important shot on each hole. But even the best players take more strokes with their putter than with any other club, as much as (and sometimes more than) 40 percent of a round. It's most important, therefore, that you have a putter (or two) with which you are very, very comfortable.

Some putters are hotter than others. What happens is that manufacturers take putters to pro tournaments and gradually persuade more and more pros to try them. With a few exceptions, pros are inveterate tinkerers, or they'll be putter addicts (Arnold Palmer, I'm told, has more than a thousand), and if they're not too busy working on something, they might try out the new club. If they play well, other pros will see them—a couple of dozen players could be on a practice tee at a tournament at any one time—and before you know it, the new putter is on national television, literally creating a new market. It happens all the time.

Broadly speaking, putters can be categorized into blades, center-shafted, long-shafted, mallet, and other.

Blades

These are putters on which the shaft connects to the clubhead at the heel. Ben Crenshaw probably is the most prominent blade user.

Center-Shafted

A history lesson: Walter Travis used a center-shafted "Schenectady" putter to win the British Amateur in 1904—and the Brits immediately banned it. But they soon reneged,

and it's just as well they did because most of the classic putters, such as the Ping Anser or the Spalding Bullseye, have
had their shafts connect to the head somewhere between
the heel and the toe. Some have heads slightly offset, others
have high hosels, some actually connect to the clubhead
pretty near the heel, but the principle is the same.

Long-Shafted

There is much debate over the validity of these putters. Those against them argue that as long as you anchor
the grip, and therefore the shaft, into your chest or—and
this is less prevalent—your chin, then you are fundamen-
tally altering the nature of the swing. I agree, and for that
reason I don't think long putters should be allowed in the
game. I have no problem with their length. But when
they're anchored to the game they're crossing a line, in the
same way that side-saddle putting is fine but standing
astride the line to putt is not. I discourage amateurs from
using long putters.

Mallet Putters

The most popular mallet over the years has been the
Ram Zebra. They have semi-circular mallet heads and
lines on the top that both give the clubs their names and
help with alignment. They tend to be very flat putters,
which is to say that, when you take your stance, your eyes
tend to be pretty far behind the line. I'm one of those putters who prefers to have his eyes directly over the line of
the putt at address.

Other Putters

There have been more crazy designs for putters than for any other clubs, and a lot of them are flat-out rejected by the United States Golf Association, which monitors equipment standards. But this isn't what we mean by "other." We instead mean such clubs as the center-shafted model with an oversized head that became immensely popular after Jack Nicklaus won the 1986 Masters with one.

No matter which putter you chose, you should be careful to make sure that its sole lies flush to the ground when you address the ball. It's the same as with irons: if the toe is off the ground at address, you need a flatter lie on your putter. Ditto if the heel is of the ground at address: Move upright.

BALLS—IT'S NOT JUST DIMPLES

There are few golf balls that can be called bad, principally because golfers are aware of their options and will switch quickly from a ball with which they're uncomfortable. So the market tends to be very competitive.

Broadly speaking, you have the big guns like Titleist and Spalding that own most of the market and keep reminding golfers why everyone plays their balls, and you have smaller ball manufacturers fighting for the scraps. These are the companies who scream longer and straighter, or boast about new golf-ball technology or materials.

I can't say that any single ball will take strokes off your game, but I can say that the top players prefer balls

Just One Ball

If you play in tournaments, you should be aware of the one-ball rule. During a round you are not allowed to change brand or model. So be smart: Make sure to carry only one type of ball—and have a good supply.

that spin more (they're easier to maneuver and to stop closer to the hole) and those that have greater feel. We tend to gravitate therefore to balls with softer covers. Traditionally, this was balata, a natural substance, but so many synthetics now have so much feel that there are many more options.

Feel is tremendously important in a golf ball, and I believe that ultimately—despite an increasing desire for distance—it is what drives the choice of ball. It's important on short shots around the green in that it helps a golfer's touch and it's also important on long shots because it can give you feedback on both good and bad shots.

Balls also come in different compressions, the most popular being 90 compression (but you'll also find 80 and 100). This measures the amount the ball flattens against the clubface at impact—the more it compresses, the more bounce it has, and therefore the farther it will fly. Not to confuse the issue, but the higher the number, the less the ball compresses—or rather, more weight would have to be applied to the ball to compress it. Top professionals use a high compression—100—because they have faster swing speeds that can compress the ball, and the lower compressions tend to be too soft. That was, for years, the conventional wisdom. Lately a lot of players have switched to 90 compression and have found they get greater feel, especially on short-iron shots, when they don't swing hard, and a 100 ball would give very little feedback. So unless your game analysis suggests otherwise, you should be perfectly content with 90 compression.

Despite the fact that most golf balls are good golf balls, there is a progression to follow as you get better. When you start out with scores, you're better off using a ball that doesn't fly far but will roll farther on impact, and with synthetic covers, because they're harder and won't get torn up by bad swings (such golfers aren't called hackers for nothing). As you improve you'll graduate to a ball that spins more, giving you a greater choice of shots, and has a synthetic cover and a 90 compression. The last stop is balata cover, plenty of spin, and 90 compression.

But, as noted, I can't say that one ball is significantly better than another. Put another way, what (and who) hits the ball matters much more than the ball itself.

GETTING FITTED

While some companies sell off the rack, some companies specialize in clubfitting, similar to tailors that specialize in made-to-measure suits. Whatever you prefer is less important than making sure all the specifications are correct. You should cover all the points I mentioned when discussing the elements of equipment (lies, shaft flex, etc.), while taking into consideration your height, leg length, arm length, torso length, swing speed, typical ball flight, and the shape of your swing. As we've discussed, no two swings are the same, but the aim is the same for every golfer—consistent and correct ball flight on every swing, with every club.

It's also a good idea to have your professional check your specifications at least once a year. When you consider that most golf shots involve slamming the club into the ground at 100 mph, you can understand how they can get knocked out of shape.

GLOVES AND SHOES

Correct glove size is important. After all, you wouldn't play wearing a hat that was too large, would you? Your glove should be snug without being tight, because looseness means extra material inside your grip—not a good idea. You also should change gloves at the slightest sign of wear. But if you find that you're changing a little too often, then you should check your grip pressure. If the pad of your glove is wearing down then you could be gripping the club too near the butt end and allowing it to wobble during the swing. And if the back end is wiggling, you know that the clubhead is wiggling, too.

Wearing a glove is a matter of choice. I happen to believe that it anchors the left hand better than a bare hand would, and that's important. It also helps to have a tacky surface on the club. But overall it's a matter of personal choice.

TENDER LOVING CARE

Car owners tend not to let their vehicles fall into disrepair. They wash them, clean out the insides, change the oil, put them in for regular service. And what do families do with dishes they just used for dinner? They wash them, dry them, and store them.

At least the same devotion should be administered to your golf clubs. They are, after all, the tools of your trade. And they should be maintained not only because clubs in good condition perform better. There's a financial benefit in that clubs kept in good condition don't have to be replaced so often.

After each round you should wipe your clubs with a damp cloth and towel them dry. Clean out each and every groove. Scrub the grips with hot, soapy water and towel dry. And always check for any damage.

As for shoes, brush off any dirt and such, polish, and insert shoe trees. Change your spikes, metal or soft, regularly. I won't offer any advice on which shoes to wear, other than stating that they should be comfortable and have spikes in good condition. After all, the swing, as my esteemed colleague Jack Nicklaus has often said, begins from the ground up.

3

The Well Golfer...............

It's all very well being able to hit good golf shots, but if you are not of a sound mind and body, if you are not a true "well golfer," then your ability to improve will suffer immeasurably.

Essentially, the concept of a well golfer can be broken down into three areas:

1. Mental fitness (and toughness)
2. Physical fitness
3. Diet and nutrition

Improve these three areas and you will increase your flexibility, your stamina, and your mental acuity or sharpness. This will benefit you not only during a single round, but throughout your entire golfing life.

MENTAL FITNESS

It was Ben Hogan who said that golf was 80 percent mental and 20 percent physical. Hogan's numbers might even have been conservative. It's true that golf is more a game of making the correct decisions on the golf course than it is of actually striking the ball, but mental fitness is necessary in other areas of the game, too.

Let's say, for example, that you set yourself a strict diet regimen. If you've spent your life eating fast-food hamburgers, it's going to take quite an act of willpower to switch to poached chicken breast—and keep doing it for the long term.

Or let's say that you run into some nasty traffic problems while driving to your club for an important match. The golfer who is not mentally prepared to deal with this will arrive at the club—assuming he gets there on time—angry and in no shape to play golf, never mind play well. The golfer who is mentally fit, on the other hand, will pull out of the traffic, call ahead to alert the club to his problem, and perhaps work out a different route to travel. He stays calm.

But probably the most important area in which you should be mentally fit concerns visualization.

You can read a lot of advice about visualizing the shot before it is hit. Some amateurs think this is some kind of odd, Zen-like thing. Yet most do it routinely before striking a putt. Tour pros do it, albeit to different degrees. It usually begins when we're walking to our balls. We already know how we want to play the hole, so if we've hit our tee shots to where we intended, we can start thinking about the next shot. If we haven't, then we can draw from previous experience to start visualizing what we want to do next. I usually allow myself the luxury of thinking about other things once I've hit the ball and am on my way to the next shot, but within 10 or 15 seconds of getting to the ball, or when I put my glove on, all thoughts turn to the matter at hand: I start to imagine and visualize the shot, and my hitting the ball.

Once my caddie and I reach the ball, we go through a series of checks. We reacquaint ourselves with the green-side area. Then we check the lie, and our yardage book, and, of course, the weather conditions, particularly the wind. When we've determined where we want to hit the ball and what the yardage is, I start deciding on the shape of shot. This is where visualization comes in. On most shots I don't really see the ball leaving the clubface or see some imaginary line to the target. It's fainter than that, more of a feel thing. But it really depends on the shot.

Without wanting to dispute the value of visualization, I will say this: You should not expect to get the most out of visualizing a shot before first really understanding ball flight. And ball flight is something I don't think most players truly understand.

Here's what I tell them: Go out to the woods, find a tree that is high enough and with enough branches, and then start hitting balls at it. Find out which club you need to get over the tree, which club flies a ball between a particular pair of branches, which club flies it *under* certain branches. You're using the tree as a frame of reference and soon you will have a better understanding of ball flight. Only then can you use visualization to your maximum advantage.

It's also a good idea to start visualizing how you will play as you travel to the course (perhaps when you're stuck in all that traffic). Unless you're about to play a course with which you are not in the least bit familiar, there will be certain key holes that you may want to concentrate on. A tough par four with water cutting in from the left. You can visualize your tee shot coming to rest safely away from the water yet in good position to hit to the green (normally the best position is the one closest to the danger).

Another way to visualize play before starting a round is to pre-play in your mind the entire course. Certainly you cannot anticipate weather conditions when you do this, but it does help you prepare mentally for the round ahead.

One of the things that visualization can help with is getting rid of negative thoughts. You won't be so quick to start ticking off all the dangers on a hole if you already have played that hole safely, albeit in your mind, several times before. You have to think positively.

Positive thinking is something that all good golfers possess. Even those who languish far down the money list don't show up thinking they're going to miss the cut. There will be times when making the cut will be a goal, but every touring professional knows that he or she is able to win, because it was only through winning they got their status in the first place.

I'm no different from anyone else playing the Senior or regular Tour. When I show up it's because I plan to win, and see no reason for not being able to do so (or for thinking that way; golf fans pay good money to watch us play). In the 1974 U.S. Open, later dubbed "The Massacre at Winged Foot" because of the testing conditions and the ensuing high scores, I knew that just because

I was having trouble breaking par—I did it only in the second round—there was no reason to think negatively. That was because everyone was having trouble with what Bobby Jones (himself a winner at Winged Foot) once called "Old Man Par." I figured that if I could survive better than anyone else, then I'd win, and that was what happened.

Of course, there will be days when the music just isn't playing, and these must be treated positively, too. You should understand that no one hits superb shots all the time, and making the most out of what's working is a tremendously positive thing. If, for instance, you were set free in a fully stocked kitchen and asked to cook up something wonderful, it's reasonable to expect you to do just that. But if I hand you a couple of oranges, what's the best thing to do? Make a tasty glass of fresh-squeezed orange juice, of course.

This sort of thing happened to me on the 1998 Senior Tour, when I was playing the Bank of Boston Classic in late August. There was nothing particularly good about my game at the time—perhaps I was mentally off from playing and traveling so much—but I figured I'd just stick it out and try not to make too many mistakes. Just keep working the ball towards the hole, stay out of trouble, think as positively as possible, and hope that a putt or two would drop. This approach showed in my scores of 69–64–68 for a 15-under-par total of 201 (how can you not think positively about an under-par total?).

Another example of positive thinking is one we've touched on already. In the 1998 U.S. Senior Open at Riviera, I began with a 77. I was way off the pace. One way to enhance positive thinking is to flush bad rounds, bad holes, bad experiences out of your system. Forget about them. It's not always easy to do. It's been said that Arnold Palmer was never the same after losing a seven-stroke lead to Billy Casper in the final nine holes of the 1966 U.S. Open (which Billy then won in a playoff). That Tony Jacklin never recovered after Lee Trevino pulled himself off the mat to chip in and win the 1972 British Open. I can't speak for either of these fine golfers but I sympathize with them if it's true.

At Riviera, the first thing I did after checking and signing my scorecard was leave the scorer's tent and start the Senior Open campaign afresh. People, the media mainly, asked me about the round and what effect did I think it would have, and I answered that it didn't matter, that it was over, behind me. I wasn't trying to be testy, or glib. It was over. I had 54 holes left to play and the only way I was going to get back in the hunt was to think positively. But how could I do that if I was rehashing what probably was the worst round I'd had since joining the Senior Tour?

That championship also ended with an example of positive thinking. As noted in the introduction, I gambled on my final approach by hitting to a pin position that was well guarded by long rough. I hit the shot partly because I felt it was time to take a risk, but also because I knew I could make the shot. And I visualized making it from almost the moment I saw where my tee shot had landed.

One of the most recent examples of the power of positive thinking was the debut of Tiger Woods on the PGA Tour. Tiger came out looking like he would sweep everything in site, winning twice in his first eight starts in 1996, winning the first event of 1997, then The Masters, and so on. But then Tiger stopped winning so much. Had he lost the power of positive thinking? I doubt it. He has said he always expects to win, and he has every right to; he certainly plays like it. It's more likely that Tiger's schedule took its toll. When you become physically tired, the mind is usually the next thing to go, and it's tough thinking positively when you're mentally burned out.

HOW YOU SEE YOURSELF

Golf is such a difficult game—albeit one that can be mastered—that many golfers suffer from terrible self-esteem. When a golfer who regularly shoots in the mid-80s is asked what he shoots, he usually says "low 80s." It's not that he has such a good impression of himself, or that he's a flat-out fibber. It's that he has low self-esteem because he shoots in the mid-80s—even though that's a perfectly good score for great number of golfers.

Likewise, golfers get into what's been called a comfort zone. That's a score they're comfortable with, and when they get in a position to lower the score considerably they put themselves under such pressure by thinking "I'm not this good" that they drop a few strokes and end up back at their usual score. Hey, that feels better.

Guess what. You *are* that good. If you're a 16 handicapper, you're good enough to be a 12 handicapper. If you're a 12 handicapper, you're good enough to be an 8. And so on. Granted, you're not going to go from 16 to 8 without a lot of work, but the very fact that your handicap is lower than a stroke a hole means that you have a foundation on which to build.

You have to start thinking this way. When you buy a new suit do you think, "I'm not good looking enough for this suit"? When you buy a nice new car, do you keep it in the garage because you don't look good enough driving it? Of course not. Yet so many golfers get themselves into a position to improve and then never come through because they subscribe to this self-defeating prophecy that they belong at a certain skill level.

This lack of self-esteem pervades different parts of your game, too. If you stand over a bunker shot and tell yourself that you're not a very good sand player, you will not hit a very good sand shot. Golfers are notorious for talking themselves out of perfectly playable shots. "My draw could be in real trouble with all that out of bounds down the left." Reload. "That water shouldn't come into play unless I hit this one fat." Wet.

Do you think it's possible that Mark O'Meara stood over his winning birdie putt on the final hole of the 1998 Masters and said to himself, "You know, I'm not a bad putter but there's a lot of pressure with this one. I'll win a major if I hole it, but I'm not a major winner." Of course he didn't. He said, "I can make this. It's time to win my first major." And the ball never left the hole.

You have to start thinking like that.

But this book should help you. As noted in the introduction, we're not preaching some new-fangled instruction technique. We believe that by playing smarter you can lower your score—and then lower it even further as you ingrain good habits. You no longer will have to carry the nagging thought that you can't break through the scoring plateau you've occupied for so long. You can start thinking of yourself as a smart golfer, and start making smart decisions on and off the golf course.

You have to start thinking like that.

TEMPER, TEMPER

Temper and smart golf just don't go together. When your mind is consumed with anger at a poorly hit shot or a bad bounce, then it can't focus on the matter at hand, which normally is the next shot. In a matter of minutes a bogey can balloon into double bogey, triple bogey, or worse.

This is a true story. When Jack Nicklaus was 11 years old, having just taken up the game, he was out on the course with his father when he got frustrated at himself— or, rather, at the way he was hitting the ball—and threw a club. "That's the last club I hope you'll ever throw," his father told him, "or that's the last hole you'll ever play." Of course Jack didn't throw another, and he certainly played many, many more holes of golf, most of them pretty well.

His father was giving him a lesson in behavior, but the point that he would never get better as long as he let his temper get the better of him wasn't lost on the boy. Temper tantrums and golf, Jack Nicklaus has proven, just don't go together.

I can't say I've never been mad on the course. I've hit a few strange shots that have had me burning up inside.

And you can ask any of my peers—I doubt if there is anyone more competitive on any of the pro tours.

I can't emphasize enough how important it is to control your emotions on the golf course. It was said that the pulse of tennis legend Björn Borg actually dropped during his big matches. Think about that. When the situation is set up for your pulse to be racing, his was slowing down. It enabled Borg to avoid the costly mistakes that so many players in every sport suffer. Golf is no different. Sooner or later players make mistakes, but the player who stays calmest and avoids mistakes usually will win. When players talk of the U.S. Open as being a test of survival, they don't mean only that you have to survive a course set up with high rough, fast greens, and fairways as narrow as shoelaces. They also mean—or, rather, they *really* mean—surviving the mental game that can lead to both mental and physical errors.

I'll be the first to admit that I'm not the most animated golfer around. I get excited in an obvious way (fist-pumping and all that) when I hole a putt that means something, and I get excited but keep it to myself when I hit a good shot during a round. But beyond that I try to keep a calm demeanor, one that will prevent me from making rash mistakes or getting uptight from the inevitable mistakes that crop up during a round.

There are two other, very important reasons why you shouldn't let your temper get to you during a round. One is that you end up looking like a complete fool. Believe me, any golfer will accommodate, even encourage, a golfer who's having a bad day and tries to work through it. Or, failing that, keeps in the background and keeps up a chipper demeanor. But the player who slams a club into the ground or curses, or even throws a club . . . that player may be thinking he's just showing honest emotion, but he's not. He's being foolish.

The second reason is that golf courses are places that are shared and enjoyed by a lot of people, and it is every golfer's responsibility to respect his fellow golfer. No one wants to see the course damaged because someone was unhappy by the way he hit a shot or chose to play a shot. Likewise, no one really wants to hear someone shouting loudly. Golfers go out to a course to enjoy themselves, so what pleasure can they possibly take from the inconsiderate actions of others?

The tough question to answer is, of course, "How do I control my emotions?" One thing I've done in the past is make a secret pact with myself. "No matter how mad I may get or how poorly I play," I tell myself, "I will not let on to my opponent or my fellow competitor how I feel." Call this playing golf like a professional poker player. Did you ever see Lee Trevino show excessive negative emotion on a golf course? Or Jack Nicklaus? I emphasize the word "negative," because although Jack is known for his calm demeanor—to paraphrase Rudyard Kipling, he keeps his head when all around others are losing theirs—he does show emotion. Those who recall the 40-foot birdie putt he holed on the 16th at Augusta National that all but clinched the 1975 Masters may also recall that he jumped up in the air, putter held high, and ran around the green in full view of his contenders.

Among the younger players, Davis Love and David Duval never seem to be bothered by a rough stretch. And

A Little Technique

This book is not about the technique of hitting a golf ball. I'm not teaching swing plane, or how to chip and pitch. But what I can tell you about technique is that there are several smart thoughts to have about how you hit the ball.

When I reach my ball and have come to various conclusions about the lie, the weather, the target, the yardage, the shape of the shot I want to hit, and the club I'm going to hit, I immediately put all those thoughts behind me and click into swing mechanics. It's not a good idea to overthink mechanics, however, because the notion of overanalysis leading to paralysis is true. So I try to simplify things.

I start with what I call good body balance. This takes in alignment, posture, and, quite literally, balance. Grip pressure also is a part of it.

Next I consider ball position. Some golfers advocate one position, but I like to move it around a little bit, further back in my stance for the shorter clubs.

Now I think solely of tempo, or how I will get the club to the proper position at the top of the backswing. However, I don't mean thinking about where the clubhead is at all times during the backswing. I believe amateurs place too much emphasis on the backswing when playing (it's fine to work on your backswing when practicing). They freeze during the backswing and are unable to "load" the club for the downswing, and forget that *the whole idea is to hit the ball.* I've seen lots of great golfers with loopy backswings—look at Miller Barber or Jim Furyk—but they all get the club into the proper position to hit the ball.

And then I just let fly, making sure I swing through the ball and not *at* it. If you hit at it you're more likely to throw the club at the ball and not swing through it. I prefer to accelerate through the ball. Tests have shown that the club is traveling fastest just before impact. Maybe that's true, but I try to make it a lie, and make the club swing fastest just after impact. It's like a sprinter trying to run flat-out for 105 meters instead of 100.

Ernie Els? He, perhaps, has the demeanor we would all die for. But there are some players who give it away immediately. You can see players slamming clubs into the ground, or throwing them at their bags, or even cussing. To me, it's far smarter to work on the poker face: whether you're sitting with four kings or a pair of eights, the look should remain the same.

In this book I advise that a golfer work on maintaining a set pre-shot routine. This is another aspect of your game that can be affected by a poor frame of mind (although I will concede that working on a pre-shot routine can calm you down). If you're still livid because you tried to force a club to where it wasn't really feasible to hit (in most cases you make your own problems, cause your own temper to boil), then unless you can shut what happened out of your mind, you won't be able to focus on preparing for the shot. Your visualization will be affected and, ultimately, so will your execution of the shot.

Now, if you're not the poker-faced type of golfer, then you have to work extra hard to prevent your emotions from affecting your game. Sad to say, I've seen a lack of emotional control destroy perfectly promising players, many of whom were perfectly pleasant human beings, and very good golfers to boot. The problem is that some golfers see the glass as half empty when others see it as half full. The half-full golfers—a fraternity to which I belong—are constantly striving for more, reaching for the stars. The half-empty guys, on the other hand, are looking for a place to wreck. People who have this attitude are prohibiting themselves from moving up the ladder. The guys who play on tour for years without winning—it's not me or Jack Nicklaus or Curtis Strange or Tiger Woods who are preventing them from winning. They're doing it to themselves. They've proven they're good enough to play on the tour, but they don't identify the opportunity to win.

An odd case may be Mark O'Meara, who won both The Masters and the British Open in 1998. Here was a guy who won on Tour regularly but never made the step up the ladder that involves winning a major. He was perfectly happy with his life—great family, enough wealth, all the comforts that come with being a successful touring professional. He didn't see the glass as half empty, but it was as if, when he stood over that putt for victory on the final green at Augusta, he suddenly saw the glass as half full. All he had to do to take himself to the next level was hole a putt! And bang—Mark O'Meara was a different golfer, a different person. It happened pretty late in his career, but at least it happened.

And what do you gain from controlling your emotions? Besides a better score, you'll enjoy the game more. If you can stay mentally strong, then the next great shot is only a stroke away. When Brooklyn Dodgers owner Branch Rickey was asked how long it would take for his move to Los Angeles to be forgiven he replied, "A four-game winning streak." Golf is not much different. Stay calm and hit a few good shots and you'll forget your problems quickly.

The last area of mental strength I'd like to address is the benefit of confidence. Remember how I said that making the cuts was a good goal when I started out because going home for the weekend was a fast way to kill your confidence? The same applies to individual shots on the golf course. If you start to make shots you'll become a more confident golfer. If you're confident that you can make a five-foot putt, you can be aggressive with longer putts in certain situations. If you're confident in your wedge game, then trying to make a world-beating shot to a tight green with a long iron may not be such a bad idea. And all the pros aim for sand when they need a bail-out area because we're all confident in our sand games (and putting).

But the best things confidence does is breed *more* confidence. It makes you feel better and think better and execute better. It's true that overconfidence is the other side of this coin, and it makes sense to heed the warning signs (don't try to thread a 1-iron through trees and land it close to a tight pin position on a green the size of a throw rug). But when you're playing with confidence, it allows you to make smart choices on the golf course, confident that you can execute the shots. That's smart golf.

THE PHYSICAL YOU

Just as the Senior Tour was taking shape, something else happened on the PGA Tour that resulted in the elderly circuit being able to trade on much more than just nostalgia: fitness vans.

These are large trailers, about the same size as the equipment vans, that inhabit one end of the practice range and allow us to work on our clubs and such. They travel from event to event and provide players with a place to stay in shape.

As simple as this is, it was revolutionary. Although there always have been players possessed of incredible longevity—Sam Snead comes to mind—most players either prolonged their careers by keeping themselves in top shape (Gary Player) or they watched their careers fizzle out as they turned 40 and patches of gray crept into their hair. What the equipment van did was make staying in shape even more convenient than having exercise equipment at home, which many players do. In addition, for some players it became a useful way to while away an hour or so of downtime, something that's pretty common on the pro tours. Inside the vans is an array of fitness equipment: stationary bicycles, Nautilus-like multi-exercise equipment, and physical fitness experts who can advise you on getting the most out of your body and answer any questions you have.

The result has been that pro golfers as a group have become fitter. There are those who believe that walking 18 holes during a round hardly constitutes a physical workout. On cool days on flat courses, when things are going well for you, that may be true. But on hot days on hilly courses, when the odd mistake can add to the baggage, then it can be tough. And as any baseball player will tell you, one mark of success is consistency over a long period, in ballplayers' cases, 162 games. In our case, consistency over a year can mean making, say, 26 cuts in a little more than 30 tournaments. That means something on the order of 116–120 competitive rounds, plus pro-ams and practice rounds, time on the practice tee, plus any outings, a few overseas appearances, practice at home, and, to put all this together, criss-crossing the U.S. and a couple of oceans several times. It's not that I'm complaining—I have, after all, made a good living from the grind—but it is true that the life of a pro golfer can amount to 200 rounds a year. If you have handicap cards from recent years, take them out and look at your number-of-rounds totals. You'll rarely find more than 100 rounds played. It's an absolute truth that the player who really wants to improve is going to have to perform better over a heavy schedule.

And that those who stay in shape have a better chance of succeeding.

What the fitness vans on the PGA Tour did for the Senior Tour, unwittingly as it may have been, was prepare its players. Those who wanted to stay in shape to compete while in their forties, suddenly found that they could keep up the good work into their fifties, when they were on the Senior Tour. Players such as Gary Player, Lee Trevino, Bob Charles, and Raymond Floyd had new leases on their golfing lives simply because they had decided to stay in shape.

The same is true for the amateur player. Not that you should aim for the Senior Tour. Rather, by staying in good physical shape, you not only will improve your current performance, but you will prolong your golfing life. You won't have a fitness van to repair to, but you should think of either fitting your own home with fitness equipment (and finding a regime to follow) or joining a club. I've also heard of more and more golf and country clubs installing fitness equipment on their premises to accommodate members who are now realizing the benefits of physical wellness. As Gary Player could rightly have said more than 30 years ago, "I told you so!"

THE PHYSICAL KEYS

Although I try to stay in shape, I won't claim to be an expert on fitness. I do general body toning, as opposed to golf-specific exercises. Working on as many muscle groups as possible leads to better overall *body* balance. Besides, golfers spend most of their time away from the golf course.

If I had to be specific, however—and a lot of other good golfers are—I'd have to say that the main things to work on, as part of overall body conditioning, are:

- flexibility
- back strength
- hip strength
- strength in the big muscles of the legs
- strong shoulders, particularly in the rotator cuff area

There are two of the above areas I want to highlight: hip strength (and flexibility) and big-muscle strength in the legs (and thighs). The former is important because it's tough to achieve a strong shoulder turn without also having strong hips. The hips are in a sense resisting the shoulder to create a sort of spring action. They are holding the torso steady while the shoulders turn, and they bear a lot of the pressure caused by the unnatural movement of the golf swing. To increase hip flexibility and strength, lie on your side on the ground and do leg lifts. Then swing your legs across your body. When this becomes too easy, add ankle weights.

You also should work on keeping the big muscles in your legs and thighs in shape because so much power and—if you are in shape—control is generated from here. Leg curls, working out on a stationary bicycle, and running all help.

There also are big muscles elsewhere in your body—in your chest, your back, your abdomen, your shoulders, your arms. To strengthen these muscles, you should do push-ups (chest, shoulder, arms), pull-ups (back, arms), squats (legs, abdominals), and sit-ups (abdominals). Sit-ups also help your back because a flat, muscled stomach is far easier for a back to support than one that is flabby and out of shape.

The Lower Back

This is the Achilles' heel of the good golfer. It is the part of the body that probably undergoes the most twisting during the golf swing. You often will hear of golfers suffering from back pain, particularly in the lumbar region (the lower back). In fact, I heard a statistic issued by the PGA and Senior PGA Tour not too long ago that said 26 percent of all injuries—not just back injuries but *all* injuries—are lower-back related. That is an astonishing number.

How does one prevent back injury? Well, periodic rest does help, but you can't expect to improve without considerable practice. And, besides, it's much smarter to practice preventative medicine than remedial medicine. I recommend forward and lateral back extensions—hands on the hips—because they not only strengthen the back muscles but also the oblique (side) abdominals and the lateral hip muscles.

Hamstring injuries are some of the worst any athlete can suffer. One reason is that they have a tendency to resurface just when you thought they were gone for good. And once this happens a few times, you become overly sensitive to it happening again, and that makes you tentative. You start swinging at 60–65 percent of your natural force, and with an even smaller percentage of your mind focused on hitting the ball. This just leads to disaster.

Stretching the hamstrings is simple and smart. Just bend and touch your toes (or get as close as possible) without bending your legs. Don't jerk or try and reach. Just stre-e-e-e-tch and hold and let yourself back up easily. It could make the difference between serious, lengthy injury and lower scores.

In closing on fitness, I'd like to touch on the dangers of bulking up. As many golf fans know, I played college football for the University of Colorado. I played as a defensive back, which meant I had to understand the fine line between putting on too much muscle and losing flexibility. For a golfer, the plan should be to tone the muscles, to keep them strong but sleek. In football you hit people, so a combination of weight, muscle mass, and strength (not to mention speed) is ideal. In golf, you must retain the flexibility that will allow you to make a full turn and a powerful follow-through. I'd recommend that you find a professional fitness trainer, and lay out for him or her exactly what your needs and goals are, and have that person design a fitness regimen for you.

And one last thing.

Don't smoke.

DIET AND NUTRITION

Note: The smart thing to do at this juncture is to turn to an expert. Fortunately, Dr. Debra Hartley (M.S., R.D.) can serve as our resident expert. She's the wife of Jim Hartley, one of the collaborators on this book.

Your diet affects you probably more than you realize. It affects how you feel, how you look, how much energy you have (and can maintain during a round), and how well you play. Certainly the last of these is critical, but the first three should not be overlooked. Without them, number four does not exist.

So it's important to have a healthy diet all the time which, for the smart golfer, means on the golf course, in the hours before a round (tremendously important), and off the golf course.

Every golfer can benefit by following the basic principles of smart eating. You should cut down on meat and use grains, rice, and pasta as the basis of a healthy diet. By grains we mean wheat, oatmeal, etc. Rice and pasta are obvious. You should eat more of these than anything.

Fruits and vegetables are the next most important foods. I'd advise against cooking vegetables too much. Raw fruit and vegetables are far healthier.

As for dairy, meat, poultry, fish, beans, eggs, and nuts, because they have higher fat content many of these foods should be eaten in moderation. I won't advocate that you avoid them, however. Think instead of a big steak as a celebration of a victory or a period of vast improvement.

Some items should be consumed only occasionally—sweets and alcohol.

A SMART GOLFER'S DIET

Golfers are people, too, so your diet really shouldn't vary from that of any other healthy person. What will vary is your caloric intake based primarily on your age and gender, the idea being to consume just enough to stay in shape and maintain a proper weight (staying in shape is nigh impossible if you're carrying too much baggage).

Active men and teenage boys can consume around 2,800 calories a day on average and maintain their weight. Less active men—perhaps those with sedentary jobs—and active women should have a daily caloric intake of no more than 2,200 calories. And older males and less active women should be looking at 1,600 calories a day.

Of course, some golfers could improve their energy level, their ability to swing a golf club and, most important, their life expectancy by losing a few pounds. In this case, an active male should restrict his diet to 2,200 or as few as 1,600 calories for a period of weeks or even months.

To ensure you get your targeted daily calorie level, consult a doctor or a registered dietitian. You then can determine how many servings of each food group you should be selecting per day. "Sample Daily Diets" on page 66 explains what one serving constitutes within each group.

While your diet will vary from day to day, it's interesting to look at how servings and food groups translate into an actual day of eating at each calorie level. In the chart on the next pages, you can see that even people on a 1,600-calorie-a-day diet can eat well if they eat smart.

GAME DAY NUTRITION

If there is one aspect common to smart golf and smart eating, it's self-discipline. A golfer faces several dietary challenges every day that he (or she) plays golf. First, there's the fact that a round of golf, plus warm-up and commute time, can add up to six or more hours. Professional golfers live with this reality five or six days a week, 30 to 40 weeks a year. So they have to learn how to eat normally despite an abnormal schedule.

For amateur golfers, who might play golf once or twice a week, it still is important to eat sensibly on a golf day. For one thing, it's likely you have other days during the week that aren't typical. So you've got to find a way to make every day one in which you can eat a balanced diet. Otherwise, you will find yourself eating too much of the wrong things too often.

Another very important reason for eating well on a day you play golf is so you can maintain your energy level throughout the entire round.

Having enjoyed a healthy pre-game meal or snack, the big test for you comes during the round. This is a real challenge, because we all know the selection at most halfway houses, snack bars, and carts: hot dogs (mustard, relish, ketchup), pre-made sandwiches loaded with butter and mayo, potato chips, danish, crackers with that orange cheese-type filling, and, of course, candy

Sample Daily Diets

1,600 cal.	**2,200 cal.**	**2,800 cal.**
Older adults, women	Most men, women	Active men, teenage boys

Breakfast

³⁄₄ cup whole grain cereal to eat)	³⁄₄ cup whole grain cereal (ready to eat)	³⁄₄ cup whole grain cereal (ready (ready to eat)
8 oz. low-fat milk	8 oz. low-fat milk	8 oz. low-fat milk
1 med. muffin	1 med. muffin	½ cup fresh straw-berries
6 oz. orange juice	6 oz. orange juice	

Snack

1 banana	1 banana	1 banana
8 oz low-fat yogurt	8 oz. low-fat yogurt	1 cinnamon-raisin bagel

Lunch

1 pita pocket sandwich stuffed with 2 oz. stir-fried chicken strips, onions, and mushrooms	1 pita pocket sandwich stuffed with 3 oz. stir-fried chicken strips, onions, and mushrooms	1 pita pocket with 3 oz. stir-fried chicken strips, onions, and mushrooms
1 apple	1 apple	1 apple
8 oz. low-fat yogurt	8 oz. low-fat yogurt	8 oz. low-fat yogurt

Snack

2 small oatmeal cookies	2 small oatmeal cookies	2 small oatmeal cookies
water	water	8 oz. low-fat milk

Dinner

3 oz. turkey meatballs in tomato spaghetti sauce	3 oz. turkey meatballs in tomato spaghetti sauce	4 oz. turkey meat-balls in tomato spaghetti sauce
1 cup pasta salad with veggies and leafy greens	1½ cups pasta salad with veggies and leafy greens	1½ cups pasta salad with veggies and leafy greens

Summary:
(in servings)

6 bread group	9 bread group	11 bread group
3 veg. group	4 veg. group	5 veg. group
2 fruit group	3 fruit group	4 fruit group
2 milk/dairy	2 milk/dairy	3 milk/dairy
5 oz. meat group	6 oz. meat group	7 oz. meat group

bars. Lots of flavor, lots of double bogeys on the way home.

Fortunately, the choices have improved in recent years. Now, you frequently can find fruit and nutritional bars, along with water and sports drinks, to complement the junk food, beer, and soda.

Let's put the choices in some perspective. Think about the last time you saw a major tournament. Any tournament, really. The days can grow long and players often stock up on snacks to keep them going during the round. Ask yourself this: When was the last time you saw a player tucking into a bacon-cheeseburger while waiting for the group ahead to clear the landing area?

Now ask yourself this: How often have you seen players munching on granola bars or other foods, such as bananas, during a round?

The answers are simple: Never to the former; frequently to the latter. And it's no coincidence that the banana eaters are playing in majors. They're smart enough to know that in taking care of their appetites they're taking care of their golf games.

So, what should the nutritionally smart golfer do? Let's start with what he or she shouldn't do. The approach I see a number of amateur golfers take is to eat a "hearty" breakfast before a morning round of golf, thinking that this will sustain them for the full round. The typical hearty breakfast? How about bacon, eggs, some hash browns, a couple of pieces of buttered toast, and a cup of coffee or two. That will sustain them all right—to the tune of about 800 calories and 56 grams of fat.

A smarter, healthier approach is to begin by eating a moderately high carbohydrate meal one to two hours before your round. Carbohydrates are the best source of food energy and include breads, pastas, grains, fruits, and vegetables. Obviously, the type of carbs you choose for your meal will be determined by the time of day you play golf. On days when you have a very early tee time, it's tough getting up early enough to have a sit-down breakfast a couple of hours before your tee time. The best option on those days is a light breakfast, followed by a healthy snack before you tee off, and something else after nine to sustain you for the last two hours. The chart on page 70 gives you an idea of how you should eat based on the time of day you tee off.

Regardless of when you play, snacks during the round

are critical for helping to maintain blood sugar, which in turn impacts your energy, concentration and even your fine motor skills. While the food selection at on-course snack shops is improving, the best bet is to bring your own snacks from home. I'm talking fruit (bananas, grapes, apples, dates, oranges, pears, raisins), trail mix, bagels, granola bars—carbohydrate snacks that are easy to carry, easy to eat, and full of energy. If you have an early tee time, get your baggie of snacks ready the night before so you'll be ready to go in the morning when you're running out the door.

It's also important to stay hydrated during the round. Golfers lose body fluids and electrolytes as they sweat. The hotter and more humid the playing conditions, the more you should drink. On a hot day, you should drink at least 8 oz. of fluid every half hour to compensate for your body's dehydration. That doesn't sound like much, but over a five-hour round it adds up to 80 oz.! In the 1998 Western Open, Greg Kraft's caddie was weak and dizzy from dehydration by the time he reached the 18th tee on the very hot and muggy Saturday round. He couldn't finish the round and was actually taken to a nearby hospital and given an IV for a few hours until he recovered.

Water is nature's best fluid to replenish the body. However, over the course of a full round of golf, and particularly on hotter days, the body needs electrolyte and energy replenishment as well. Sports drinks (Gatorade, Powerade) are found at most courses these days if you forget to bring a bottle with you.

There are two no-no's for the smart golfer, when it comes to beverages: alcohol and caffeine. In addition to

Sample Golf Day Diets

Scenario One   **Scenario Two**

Tee Time

7:15 A.M.   8:30 A.M.

Get Up

5 A.M.—make snacks for   6 A.M.—blueberry muffin
golf course   and yogurt

Leave for course

5:45 A.M.—take 1 liter   7 A.M.—take 1 liter
water, banana, apple,   water, banana, and a
blueberry muffin   cinnamon-raisin bagel

Warm-up

6:15–7:15 A.M.—eat banana,   7:30–8:30 A.M.—drink
blueberry muffin; drink   water as needed
water as needed

Front nine

7:15–9:15 A.M.—drink water   8:30–10:30 A.M.—drink
as needed   water as needed

At the turn

9:15 A.M.—orange juice and   10:30 A.M.—sports drink
toasted egg sandwich   and bagel

Back nine

9:30–11:30 A.M.—eat apple;   10:45–12.45 P.M.—eat
drink water as needed   banana; drink water as
                                 needed

Balance of day

Eat as normal   Eat as normal

Scenario Three	Scenario Four
Tee Time	
Noon	1:30 P.M.
Get up	
7 A.M.—cereal and milk, blueberry muffin, orange juice	7 A.M.—cereal and milk, blueberry muffin, orange juice
Leave for course	
10:30 A.M.—take 1 liter water, bagel with light cream cheese, apple	noon—light lunch before leaving home: turkey sandwich, yogurt, apple
Warm-up	
11 A.M.–noon—eat bagel, apple; drink water as needed	12:30–1:30 P.M.—drink water as needed
Front nine	
noon–2 P.M.—drink water as needed	1:30–3:30 P.M.—drink water as needed
At the turn	
2 P.M.—turkey sandwich (no mayo or light mayo), sports drink	3:30 P.M.—granola bar and sports drink
Back nine	
2:15–4:15 P.M.—drink water as needed	3:45–4:45 P.M.—drink water as needed
Balance of day	
Eat as normal	Eat as normal

Care for the Outside, Too

In 1998, I became National Chairman of the Eclipse Skin Cancer campaign, an educational awareness effort built around golf that was designed to alert people to the need to take *preventive* measures against skin cancer.

This wasn't a typical case of a sports celebrity lending his or her name to a worthy cause. I've been a professional golfer for more than 30 years, and my wife Sally once was a lifeguard. So we've both been exposed to the sun—as are all touring pros. That also means we know how smart it is to take care of your skin, and to heed the advice of doctors.

Did you know that almost a million new cases of skin cancer are detected in the U.S. each year? That accounts for roughly a third of all cancer diagnoses. The Skin Cancer Foundation estimates that one in six Americans will develop skin cancer at some point in their lives, and the damage starts early: for most of us, 50–80 percent of our lifetime exposure to the sun occurs before we're 18—when we're at the beach working on a tan, in the park playing Frisbee, when we're so young we think we're invincible. Of course, we're not.

It also is worth noting that interest in golf continues to rise—and that means more players are out in the sun and at risk. That's one more reason why smart golf is also about what you wear, when you play, and how you protect your body.

What follows are some suggestions that I've taken to heart over the years:

1. Use sun protection. Exposed skin must be protected. A quality sun protectant should be as much a part of your golf equipment as your glove and your shoes. About half an hour prior to going out, apply—liberally!—a sun protectant with a Sun Protection Factor (SPF) of at least 15. I use a 30. For children, whose skin tends to be more sensitive, a stronger product might be necessary. For golfers, there are non-oily sprays available to avoid a slick grip,

and waterproof skin-care products for those given to perspiring.

2. Reapply repeatedly. An 18-hole round can keep a golfer in the sun for four to five hours, and sometimes longer. The Skin Cancer Foundation recommends reapplying your protectant or a good moisturizer every two hours, more often if sweating, swimming, or towel-drying has wiped off the protectant.

3. Wear long-sleeved shirts and trousers. The sun can penetrate loose-knit clothing. Consider dark-colored pants and shirts made from tightly woven fabrics. Because I don't feel comfortable playing golf in a long-sleeved shirt, I wear a short-sleeved shirt, but the advice still is sound.

4. Wear a hat. I started out wearing a visor to protect my forehead and eyes, but I found that my head was still getting burned. I now wear a hat every time I go out to play, because having hair isn't protection enough.

5. Use a lip screen. The lips are often forgotten, but they're also a highly sensitive area, especially for children.

the obvious side-effects too much alcohol can have on your golf game, it will dehydrate you. The more you drink, the more dehydrated you become. So you drink even more, and before you know it you are dry as a desert and can hardly swing, see, or even stand properly.

Caffeine, on the other hand, impacts your central nervous system. Bad nerves for a golfer are not a good thing, especially when you're standing over a five-foot par putt that means something. A word of advice—if you value your putting stroke, lay off coffee and other caffeinated drinks before and during your round.

And that's how simple it is to stay in shape mentally

and physically. Think positively, eat and drink properly, and keep yourself in good enough shape to make the physical side of golf nothing more than a stroll in the park.

4

The Practice of Smart Golf ....

A gaping difference between the touring pro and even the top amateur golfer is the amount of time he or she is able to practice. Whereas amateur golfers can practice perhaps twice on weekends and maybe once or twice on evenings during the week—I say "can" but the truth is that most don't—the regimen of a pro golfer is different. In a typical tournament week, I practice twice a day. This assumes, of course, that my tee time, not to mention the pace of play, allows two practice rounds. I'll warm up before the round and, afterwards, I'll practice either to work on something I noticed during the round or just to wind down—if it's been a tough day, there often is nothing better than to lose yourself on the range. And sometimes we just enjoy spending time on the range. Tour pros have an actual locker room but, in another sense, the practice range is our locker room, because this is where we see the most of each other. We don't socialize, but it is the place where we talk things over and catch up with each other (more so on the Senior Tour than on the regular Tour).

This is not to suggest the practice range is play and not work. Far from it. For every minute we spend talking about something other than golf we'll spend 50 minutes working on our games. And working properly. That, in fact, may be a bigger difference between the touring pro and the amateur. When we work on the practice range, we are working with a purpose. People talk about the number of balls that Ben Hogan hit, but he was hitting quality balls, not just hitting balls. I have found that hitting 50 quality shots is far better than just hitting 500 shots for the sake of putting in the practice. We're also not trying to see how far we can hit it. Heck, we *know* how far we can hit it.

But that's one of the perplexing things about amateur golfers. Let's say I said to you, "You're going on vacation for a week. What are you going to pack?" You'd probably reply, "I'll need two jackets for evenings, three pairs of slacks, two dress shirts, five casual shirts, plenty of golf clothes . . ." You get the idea. The point is, you make sure everything is covered. Yet when most players go to the practice range, they do the same thing: they pound balls with their drivers. True, not everyone does this. There are those who have read about a tour pro's warm up, how he'll start with short irons, swinging easily, then move up through the bag to the driver (putting comes after the range, of course, except when it's cold and we run the risk of tightening up on the practice green before going out on the course). The next time you're at a practice range, either at a club or at a driving range, count the number of people who are practicing with a purpose. Then count the ball-pounders. There *always* are more pounders.

Or rather, they lose. Because their practice doesn't help them nearly as much as it should. Going to the range and pounding balls is not the smart thing to do. What is smart is working on your whole game, with emphasis on the areas in which you are weaker. You'll recall that in the chapter on setting goals we conducted an in-depth statistical analysis of our game, measuring how many drives hit the fairway, how many times we got up and down from sand, and so forth. As you continue to analyze your game, your analysis will tell you what to spend more time on. There isn't a single area of the game that you should not work on; if you constantly hit fairways, for example, you should still work on your driving because it's something you want to keep doing, but it's a smart idea to focus more on your problem areas.

A STARTING POINT

Smart golf begins with the understanding that the likelihood of your perfecting the golf swing is about nil. (Although some golfers are closer to perfection than others.) What you are working toward is implementing all the technical elements of the golf swing to the point that you consistently strike the ball properly.

Let me emphasize the term "consistently." One of the truest measures of success is the ability to perform well over and over again. This is true not only in golf but in other sports (as noted earlier, baseball's 162-game season

Practice During a Round

One time to practice that almost everyone overlooks is during a round. If you're playing in formal competition, you are permitted by the Rules of Golf to "practice putting or chipping on or near the putting green of the hole last played, any practice putting green or the teeing ground of the next hole to be played in the round, provided such practice stroke is not played from a hazard and does not unduly delay play." In other words, if there's a wait on the next tee and the hole behind you is open, putt and chip a little. If the hole behind you is not open but there is a wait on the next tee, then practice your chipping on the tee (assuming, of course, that no one is hitting).

If the competition is stroke play, you are not allowed to practice anywhere but designated practice areas. If it's match play, say a match in your club championship, then you are allowed to practice on the course beforehand. A few warm-up holes before a match may be a smart thing to consider.

is a measure of a consistently good team) and in business (the broker who consistently buys stocks that increase in value fast becomes a very rich person).

Consistency is important in golf not only because if you are going to become a good golfer it is going to take thousands of golf shots, but also because (like confidence) consistency *breeds* more consistency. When you hit a golf ball properly over and over again you develop what is known as muscle memory. When you stand over a golf ball you no longer have to remind yourself of a zillion swing keys. You can aim, focus on the shot, visualize it, and fire away. But that consistency only comes with a lot of practice.

Another objective should be to develop as many shots as possible. There are an infinite number of situations likely to be encountered on the golf course, and you should be prepared for anything. We're not talking trick shots here; not the Phil Mickelson wedge that lands behind you, for instance. But you should want to learn to hit high, soft shots as well as low punch shots, draws as well as fades, long and short bunker shots—not to mention recovery shots from buried lies—and many, many more. And when you feel that you have enough arrows in your quiver, watch a pro tournament on television or go to a tournament and watch the contestants practice and play. I'll bet you'll see several more shots you never thought of.

There is another reason to practice a lot of different shots: you'll enjoy the game more, because the ability to master the situation presented to you is one of the reasons we play this game. After all, what would you rather do: Stand on the tee of a long par three, with the wind blowing hard from the right, and wonder how the heck your natural draw is going to find the green. Or stand on the tee and figure that this is the time to start a punched fade at the right fringe?

And a good variety of shots travel well. I had to learn a completely new lexicon of shots when I first played in the British Open, for example. My first was at Royal Lytham in 1974, and it was a nightmare! I'd never played a course on which you could hit the ball down the middle of the fairway and watch it roll into a pot bunker. I'd never played a course on which you pitched approach shots far short of the green and relied on lady luck to

Two Practice Regimens

When out on tour, I generally will begin practice at least 30–45 minutes before my starting time. I start by hitting practice shots with my sand wedge, starting with short shots of about 20 yards, and then move up through the bag hitting with every other club. The following day I'll start with the pitching wedge and practice with those clubs I did not work out the day before. After that I'll hit a few pitch shots or bunker shots, and then spend the last 5–10 minutes putting.

This routine may vary slightly if I have an early tee time. Then I'll get in a second practice later in the day, after the round, and hit the clubs not used in the morning practice.

Why don't I hit every club every day? Because there's not that big a difference between the clubs, and it's just a warm-up. Having said that, there may be an occasion when I've tried to play a certain shot on the course—a fade, perhaps—and I didn't hit it. Maybe then I'll re-create that shot after the round and work on it.

My home practice is different. Here I'm more concerned with maintenance, so I practice all the parts of my game.

I rarely practice differently for different events, although there have been instances. Before the 1998 Senior Open, for example, I practiced a lot at home in St. Louis because the zoysia grass that we have is somewhat similar to kikuyu grass at Riviera, where the U.S. Senior Open was played.

bounce them forward rather than sideways. Conditions on the great old links courses are totally unlike those we find in the U.S. The turf is firm and sandy, not soft and lush. So we have to adjust our shots. I'd been told about all this, but never really believed it. Well, believe me, it was an education. I soon learned this new game, but only by practicing hard.

Another important aspect of practice is a notepad. Before each practice session, you should jot down a game plan and stick to it. After each session, you should make some notes on how the practice went. If you were constantly hitting wedges thin, then write that down. You can refer to these notes when you make your list for the next session.

If I had to summon up a proper practice plan in three words, they would be "quality, not quantity." What I mean by that is, though I encourage a lot of practice, the degree to which you improve because of your practice will be primarily due to the way you practice—the quality of that practice. So to make sure that you understand quality, I'm going to split practice into two categories: practice before play and what I'll term general practice. Both demand quality.

PRACTICE BEFORE PLAY

Practice before play can take two forms. The first has you working on a specific part of your game; if you've been having trouble in the sand, you may want to spend some extra time in a practice bunker. However, I much prefer practice before play to be consistent. Like a pre-shot routine before a single shot, I think it's a smart plan to have a pre-play practice routine. Keep the specialty practice for time between rounds, in other words. To get a handle on a good pre-play practice routine, follow my own warm-up routine (see sidebar).

My Practice Putting Regimen

When out on Tour, I start my putting practice by holing a three-footer, then a five-footer, then a seven-footer. That way I'm successful with a short stroke, then a longer one, then an even longer one. The aim is to instill in me a positive feeling, so I get the same positive feeling standing over a 30-foot putt as I would standing over a 3-foot putt.

GENERAL PRACTICE

How much quality you can put into your practice will make or break you as a golfer. Some general guidelines. First, treat every full practice shot as though it's a real shot. By that a I mean going through your pre-shot routine, picking out a target, checking your grip, stance, address, posture, and ball position. You also should look at your ball flight to see if what you intended to do actually happened, or to study the ball and gain feedback if it did not.

You'll notice that I said every *full* practice shot. That's because there are a couple of drills I'd recommend for you that do not constitute full shots.

1. Practice hitting balls with your feet together. This is a very good exercise for working on your tempo. Don't try to crush the ball. Just concentrate on making crisp, clean contact.

2. Practice hitting with your right arm only. Much is made of keeping the right side out of the swing. Probably too much. This drill allows you to get the

feel of "hitting" the ball. And while you may think it would encourage wrist action, it actually discourages it. You have to keep your wrist firm to prevent the clubface from closing.

Another good exercise is to keep your practice balls away from you. Too often golfers just dump a pile of balls down on the ground a few feet in front of them. They hit, drag another over, hit, and so on. By putting the balls away from you, you will have to break away from your stance after each practice shot, walk over, and then come back and start your pre-shot routine. You also will get a small rest and a little time to think about your swing.

Last, always loosen up before practicing. Stretch your entire body, not just your torso and arms. The rest of your body can't swing freely if your legs are stiff.

The average golfer is estimated to return a score in the mid- to high 90s, which, roughly speaking, is made up of 14 drives, four other tee shots, eight fairway wood shots, 12 long- and middle-iron shots, eight full short-iron shots, 10 pitches and greenside iron shots, six recovery shots (including bunker shots), and 36 putts. Your practice should reflect this breakdown unless your game analysis tells you otherwise. If, for example, you consistently hit long- and middle-iron shots well but drivers poorly, then spend more time on the latter.

You should also be aware that as you improve, the ratios will change slightly, but you will probably continue to have 14 drives and four other tee shots.

Let's do some math. How many shots in that breakdown can be practiced on the range? Correct. Forty-six.

Less than half. Yet where are most golfers inclined to spend most of their practice time? Correct again. On the range.

The truth is that more time should be spent working on the short game. You should work on pitches and chips and sand shots as well as putting, because a complete short game separates pros from even the top amateurs. It's not only that we can putt better (even though we spend so much time practicing putts that it's a safe bet). No, we know from experience that we have to get our greenside shots so close we have a good chance at making putts.

Try this. Hit a dozen practice sand shots and see how often you make the putt. I'll bet you made more putts by hitting the sand shot closer. If it's not an absolute rule, it's a statistically safe assumption.

So that's the breakdown. Spend about 45 percent of your time on the range, warming up through the bag then working on the areas that your game analysis suggests need work. Spend 55 percent of your time on or around the practice green. It's safe also to assume that there will be occasions when you have only limited time to practice. This is an issue for many people these days, especially when they must combine their efforts to become a better golfer with trying to build a better business and spending more time with their family. So if time is limited, spend it at the short-game practice area.

I also would not overlook the thought of playing a quick round at an executive course. Grab a few clubs and head out. It won't take long, a couple of hours at the most, and you'll be able to work on your game from 150 yards in.

The Best Shot I Ever Hit

Elsewhere in this chapter, I talk about how practicing different shots on the range will help you out on the course. Here's an example of a shot I was able to play because I had practiced similar shots on the range. It easily rates as one of the best shots I've ever hit.

It happened on the 18th hole at Inverrary Country Club in Ft. Lauderdale, in the final round of the Honda Inverrary Classic. I'd begun the final round (because of rain we played 36 holes on the last day) three strokes behind George Burns, but birdied five holes to reach the 18th tied with Burns and Tom Kite.

The last place you want to hit the ball off the 18th tee at Inverrary is off the right side of the fairway, into trees. But that's exactly what I did. I had 153 yards to the hole and although there wasn't much rough to deal with—it was almost fairway, in fact—several trees stood between me and the pin. I had to hook the ball around the first tree but keep it low enough to stay under the branches of a tree beyond that. Once I'd determined that a 5-iron would do that, I had to figure out what the ball would do both when it approached and reached the green. There was a slight rise in front of the green. The grain of the fairway grass was running from left to right, which meant that, as the ball would be hooking into the grain, it would kill it some. That would mean the ball would be rolling up the rise, and that was important because, if it were bounding, it would go through the green.

I hit it to about six feet, and made the putt for birdie, a 65, the victory, and the 72-hole course record of 19 under par.

That was an example of thinking everything through to the minutest detail. Pros don't always think in such detail but in this situation it was the smart thing to do.

Practice Putting Drills

The drills I described above are good practical drills, what you might call situational drills. But there are a couple of good drills to practice your technique.

1. The actual stroke of your putt should be straight back, straight through. A good way to practice this is to lay down two pieces of wood, each parallel but pointing along the line of the putt, one behind your putter, one in front of the toe. Swing back and through—with or without a ball—making sure that you do not touch the wood.

2. As the perfect pace for a putt is said to carry the ball 12–18 inches behind the hole (if you try to die putts in you'll soon be coming up short), lay a club down no more than 18 inches behind the hole, then try and roll putts so that they come to a rest barely touching the club.

There is one school of thought that says that if you can't hit a certain shot, then no amount of practice will help you. You should practice, therefore, what you're good at. I'm not sure I would attend that school. I believe you should practice every part of your game and concentrate most on the weakest parts, but not if it means spending less than 55 percent of your time on your short game. Identify—using your game analysis—what practice range areas are your weakest and practice those, and do likewise for your short-game weaknesses.

On the Tour we practice because we enjoy it and because we know we have to. But for professionals the spoils include success at the highest level, respect from your peers, and a lot of money. For even the good amateur the rewards are a bit less—no offense meant. So I completely understand the amateur who complains of having to practice because the payoff might not be enough.

But without practice there is absolutely no payoff at all. So I suggest that golfers who find themselves in this situation try playing practice games. Such as these:

- Assign each shot a mark from zero, which would be a bad mishit, to three, which would be almost perfect. Hit five shots then do the math. Try to get to 10 or higher. When you can make 10 easily and consistently, raise the bar to 12. Once you can hit 12, raise it to, well, 15.

- Try hitting different shots with the same club. See how many you can come up with. As noted, not trick shots. Say to yourself, "High draw" and hit. "Low punch" and hit. At some point you will need to use some of the shots you come up with.

- This one's similar to the above game. Try to hit half your average distance with a particular club. If you hit your driver 240, hit it 120. Your 7-iron goes 150? Hit it 75.

- I know this sounds like kid's stuff, but try to imagine you're in a major professional situation when you hit shots. Eighteenth hole at Augusta National. The drive must start off straight, at the set of bunkers to the left of the fairway, and then fade to stay right of them. It also must stay out of the trees to the right. Or, you must get up and down out of sand to win the U.S.

Open. Got to hit it close. Has it ever happened? Andy North did it at Cherry Hills in 1978. Curtis Strange did it to get into a playoff with Nick Faldo at The Country Club in 1988. Although Curtis won in a playoff, the bunker recovery was a crucial shot, and he was able to pull it off—he hit it to inches—because, as was the case with Andy North, it was something he'd practiced over and over.

PUTTERING AROUND

A question: What are we trying to achieve when we practice on the putting green. A better stroke? A feel for the greens we may be about to play? The ability to hole more putts?

If you answered "Yes" to any of these then you are correct—but you are also wrong in that what we want to achieve *more than anything* is confidence.

Putting, more than any other part of golf, is a mind game. If you don't believe you can make putts then, believe me, you won't. But you don't just start believing that you can hole more putts, because if your technique is faulty, or if you have trouble reading greens, then you'll start to miss putts and no amount of whistling in the graveyard will help you. You have to work on the technique, and then apply it when you practice.

The key area to work on is from 10 feet and closer. Why not farther away, since it seems obvious that a 10-footer is easier to hole than a 20-footer? For two reasons: The first is that holing from 10 feet and in means you are holing putts you expect to hole. It's when you miss a lot

Where You Should Practice

Great piano players don't practice in a crowded room, and neither should you. Having first found a good practice facility— it could be at a local club or a driving range (a misnomer in many cases these days)—you either should find a quiet area where you can focus, or else find out when the facility is quietest, and practice then.

Practice is a very personal process. It's not about having a conversation with the golfer at the next station. It's not about listening to an instructor giving a lesson nearby. Or, rather, it is if you don't really want to use your practice to improve.

Practicing at home is not something to overlook, either (but it should not replace practicing at proper facilities). There are several worthwhile things you can do.

1. Practice your grip on a cut-down club. Just grip and regrip as you watch television.

2. Putt into a glass. Better still, a proper putting machine.

3. Practice opposite a full-length mirror. Check your wing span before swinging indoors, however.

4. Check ball position and alignment on a tiled floor. It's like stepping onto a grid.

5. Study a videotape of your swing. Use your VCR's bells and whistles, too. Freeze the frame. Slow-mo. You also could watch an instructional videotape.

6. Read an instructional book. Yes, you already are.

7. Build a practice net and hit into it (assuming you have space, indoor or out). You won't be able to study ball flight, but at least you'll get the feel of crisp contact.

8. Hit plastic balls. The classic is the Whiffle, but there are many others available. They're no substitute for the real thing, of course.

Seeking Professional Help

There are two reasons why it's a smart idea to get help from a PGA of America–credited instructor. One is that, while you may improve without the help of an expert, you may not improve as much as you could. An outside, expert eye may spot a flaw in your swing, or may suggest something you haven't even thought of.

The other reason is to keep you swinging (and playing) smoothly once you do reach close to your full potential.

A few things to keep in mind when taking lessons:

1. Practice as soon as possible after the lesson, while the advice is fresh in your mind.

2. Take notes.

3. Ask the instructor to show you what he's saying if you do not clearly understand it.

4. Always use your own clubs. It's not just that if you didn't you'd be going out on the course with different weapons, but also because a lot of instructors read ball flight to determine what to teach. They can't give good advice if they're reading something that is not your normal ball flight.

5. Do not persist with a professional who you do not completely trust, or if your personalities are just not in sync. Move on to someone else.

6. Do not assume that if you are a male golfer then you have to go to a male instructor. Same goes for females.

of these putts that your confidence erodes. The second is that you don't face as many 20-foot putts during a round as you do much longer putts—and I'll deal with lagging shortly—and the shorter ones. As we noted earlier, your practice should concentrate on quality, not quantity, and practicing the putts you are most likely to face really adds to the value of the session.

If you want to practice short putts, I recommend you start by holing three consecutive putts of about 12 inches. Before you argue that no one misses such tap-ins, remember that you're hearing this from someone who whiffed a six-incher in the 1983 British Open at Royal Birkdale—then finished one stroke out of the lead!

When you've done that successfully, move back a foot, and keep putting from there until you hole three in a row. And so on, back to ten feet. I'd also recommend that you do this exercise from as many different angles as possible. Straight uphill, straight downhill, uphill breaking left, uphill breaking right, downhill breaking left, downhill breaking right.

Lag putts are absolutely crucial putts. You shouldn't expect to hole them, but you should want to get them so close as to make the second putt routine. I'll give you some tips on lag putting in another chapter, but for practice purposes you should treat lag putts as you would during play: working more on the speed of the putt than the line. And, as with short putts, practice on as many different terrains as possible, moving on only when you can roll three consecutive putts within two feet of the hole.

And don't restrict your putting practice to the putting green. It's not as if the green is the only place you use your putter. Practice from the fringe—again from as many different angles as possible—and from where the fringe meets the rough. This last putt may seem rare, but it's not. Most amateurs do not spin the ball hard enough to stop every good approach on the green. Balls that do roll

The Smartest Practice Move I Ever Made

During the Canadian Open in 1970, I found myself unable to concentrate on my practice or play. So I felt I should give my mind a rest. Still wearing my street shoes, and without any golf equipment, I went out to the practice tee. I wanted to watch how *other* players practiced, and try not to get wrapped up in my own problems.

When you watch others, you tend to forget your own idiosyncrasies and you begin to think in broader patterns. You watch swing tempo, ball position.

I've heard the great baseball player Tony Gwynn say how he goes to minor-league ball games when he's out of sync, to watch the young, raw players swinging, and that he inevitably picks up an idea here or there.

He knows what I have come to realize: that even though you've had a career in which you've sort of seen it all and done it all, you must still be willing to learn.

through the green, and are not traveling fast enough to bounce into the rough, will come to rest on the fringe but against the rough. This is more valuable practice than you may at first imagine.

You also should have a pre-shot routine for putting. As with the longer shots, you should visualize the putt going into the hole, its speed and break. You should take one or two practice swings, perhaps looking at the hole. You should have an order in which you do things. Whether you take your stance and then ground the club behind the ball or vice-versa is up to you, but you should be consistent.

PART TWO..........................

..........................Smart Course Management

5

Preparing and Playing Smart..................

PREPPING TO PLAY AND GENERAL STRATEGY

I cannot overemphasize the need for preparation before a round of golf. You must be prepared mentally, physically, and nutritionally—and you must have with you all the proper equipment and such. No stone should go unturned.

A good way to make sure you have everything is to have a checklist—a written one, not one you keep in your head. There are those who accuse people who make lists of being pedantic, obsessed with the list more than they should be. This may or may not be true, but it is not the case with the smart golfer. A written list—a "punch list" is another name for it—makes preparation for play so much easier.

Here's what your checklist should include:

- **Fourteen clubs.** That's the maximum you're allowed. Before each round, count them and make sure they're the 14 clubs that you have determined will work best for the course or other conditions you are about to play.

- **Balls.** Make sure, as we noted in our equipment chapter, that they are all from the same manufacturer and are the same model, in terms of the name of the ball, its construction, and its compression. While you're at it, check that you have the same balls in different numbers. Here's why. Let's say you feel that "3" is your lucky number. You carry the same make, same model, and every ball is numbered "3." You're on the last hole of a match. All even. You hit a long drive that flies a bit close to the out-of-bounds line. You're smart enough to know the proper procedure when this happens, so you announce to your opponent that you intend to hit a provisional. You take another ball out of your bag, and hit it. It, too, flies pretty close to the out-of-bounds line, but you figure this one has stayed safe. When you reach the area in which you're pretty sure the first ball landed, you find a ball. Your make, your model, and the number you were playing, a "3." You tell your opponent that this was your first ball. Before you play it, your opponent finds another ball. It's the same make, same model and, yes, it has a number "3" on it. He asks if this could be your first ball. You concede that it could be, but probably isn't. Now you're in deep trouble. As your opponent knows, unless you can identify a ball as yours beyond doubt, then you must declare it lost. The big problem here is that you cannot positively identify either of the balls; who knows how they bounced and rolled upon landing? In this situation, because you did not have the foresight to play a differently numbered ball, you must return to the tee and hit your fifth shot. So much for the match.

As for how many balls to carry, bring an ample supply. Don't feel that a dozen is an insult to your skill level. Even pro golfers have been known to run out of balls in top competition. (It happened to a golfer trying to qualify for the 1998 British Open.) Losing balls is not the only reason you go through them. Any time you hit a tree, a cart path, a rock, or catch a ball thin, you may damage it to the extent that you can legally replace it. I generally change balls every three holes, unless my ball is so badly damaged that I should take it out of play—and that doesn't happen too often—or if things aren't going well and I just want to do *something* to change the atmosphere.

- **A felt-tip pen or other permanent marker to mark your ball.** The mark you make—a dot, a cross, a smiley-face—will identify a ball as yours beyond any doubt.

- **Tees.** Easy to overlook, but make sure you have at least one for each hole. Two dozen should do you fine.

- **Ball marks.** I use a coin. You can use a coin or a plastic mark. I'd caution against using the ball mark that you find buttoned into a golf glove. They have tendency to stick to your hand when you put them down, which means you could end up marking a ball in the wrong place.

- **Gloves.** I use one a round in good weather, and more in either wet weather or in conditions so hot my hands or arms sweat. It's also not a bad idea to carry one or two all-weather gloves, although in wet weather you should try at all costs to keep a leather glove dry using other methods (removing it and storing it in a dry place between shots, for example).

- **Rain gear.** Speaking of wet weather, you should carry rain gear no matter the weather conditions or the forecast. After all, weather predictions are just that: predictions. Here's a good wet-weather wardrobe: an extra set of shoes (preferably with waterproof lining); a water-repellent rain suit; a large umbrella (check periodically that it's in good shape); a few gloves; at least two towels; a rainproof cover for your bag (your clubheads will get wet when you use them in wet weather, but you should cover your bag to make sure your grips stay dry).

- **A ball repair tool.** A proper one, too. You'll see pros repair ball marks with tees, and while that can be done, it makes much more sense to carry a proper repair tool. You also should repair your ball marks by leveling the ground all around your ball, not just where it made the dent in the green. The impact of a ball also "bulldozes" the green surface into a little rise; this should be leveled, too.

- **A copy of the Rules of Golf.** A smart golfer will know the Rules already, but it's a sound idea to carry a rule book either to back up your own procedures, or to point out a procedure to an opponent or fellow competitor.

- **A yardage book.** Familiarize yourself with each hole, but don't spend so much time referring to the yardage book that you slow up play. It's not a bad idea to make your own yardage book for your own course. On Tour, we get special yardage books that give us distances to and from just about every "landmark" on the course. You can't expect to get that wherever you play, but you can certainly make one for your home course from an existing book.

- **Notes on the course you're about to play.** Refer to them before teeing off on each hole, and if you're ever in doubt before hitting a shot.

- **Snacks.** As noted in our chapter on good nutrition, what you eat on the course will affect how you play.

- **An extra scorecard or two,** to track your statistics or make other notes.

THE FIRST TEE

So off we go. The first tee. The first real shot of the day. This is one of the most interesting parts of the day

Poor Weather Smarts

It's important to know what inclement weather will do to your game, so you can adjust appropriately.

Wind. Obviously your ball will not travel as far when hit into the wind, and we've gone over how it's important you do not try to hit harder when playing in such conditions. But it also is important to know the effect of the wind on both carry and roll. Did you know, for example, that a ball can hook or slice several times more when hit into the wind than when hit with the wind?

Side wind also can be problematic. Consider the shape of your shot, the strength of the wind and its likely effect, and any danger that the wind may blow your ball toward.

Rain. First and foremost: Keep your grips dry in wet weather. If you cannot keep a firm grip on the club, whatever effect the rain may have on the impact and flight of your ball probably won't matter. It's a good idea to carry several gloves.

Next, accept that you will lose distance in wet weather because you must swing easier and you will lose both carry and roll.

Finally, if faced with what might normally be a long-iron shot, try to hit a fairway wood (and be sure your club makeup for the day—you already checked the weather forecast—includes a few extra fairway woods). Irons tend to dig into soft, wet ground easier than fairway woods, which can lead to hitting fat.

Hot weather. You should be more concerned with your physical (and therefore mental) condition than your golf game. Drink a lot of water. Wear lightweight, light-colored clothes (dark colors in colder weather). Don't spend too much time on the practice range—what you think you'd gain by practicing, you'll lose from fatigue.

Cold weather. Same message here, but different procedures. Now you want to put in a little extra practice to warm up (literally) and loosen up. You probably will need heavier clothing, but don't wear something that restricts your motion.

because it sometimes involves the toughest and most important decision.

Obviously you want to get safely off the tee. The worst way to start the day is to lose a ball left or right or in any trouble directly in front of you. And you never want to play down the importance of the first shot by saying that there's time to make it up if something goes wrong.

But we're getting ahead of ourselves. First, do you have a goal for the round? Are you trying to shoot a score? Is there an area of your game you want to focus on? Are you trying to win a match?

Next, do you have a swing thought for the round? The common denominator for all golfers is tempo, so I advise every golfer, no matter their skill level, to think tempo—the smooth transition from backswing to downswing—as the primary swing thought. Believe me, there are a lot of things you could single out in the golf swing that could become swing thoughts, but tempo tends to take care of just about all of them. Beyond that, if you want to add a swing thought, add no more than one. It could be grip pressure, proper alignment, or a short-game thought. But whatever it is, make sure it is preceded by tempo.

Then, did you remember to mark your ball as yours? And did you tell your playing partner or opponent (or fellow competitors, in stroke play competition) what make and number of ball you are playing?

Have you established who's away? In formal competition, you should always play in turn because it's against the rules of golf to deliberately do otherwise. In informal

Hilly Lies

Here's a simple chart to tell you the effect of hilly lies. Bear in mind that the degree of hilliness will multiply the effect of the hill on your shot. The chart also is for right-handed golfers only.

Lie	Ball Flight	Compensate
Uphill	Ball will fly higher	Take one more club
Downhill	Ball will fly lower	Take one less club
Ball Above Feet	Ball may fly left	Take two extra clubs, swing gently,* aim right
Ball Below Feet	Ball may fly right	Take one extra club, swing gently,* aim left (by holding the club)

*The extra clubs are not to compensate for lost distance. They're intended to *force* you to swing gently and thereby maintain your balance on the slope.

Note: The chart above comprises generalities. You may find in these situations that different things happen, and the degree to which you compensate depends on the severity of the slope (not to mention your lie, weather conditions, and such). Two key things to remember are that if you are hitting an uphill shot you should have a deeper backswing and a shallower follow-through, and on a downhill shot you should make a shorter backswing and a lower follow-through.

competition, you may want to go ahead when ready; just make sure everyone in your group understands this.

Finally you can hit. Basically, you have three priorities on the first shot.

1. **Put a good swing on the ball.** If you had time to warm up, this was what you were working toward, so why not put it to use immediately?

2. **Keep the ball in play,** even if that means clubbing down to a 3-wood or an iron. It's important to understand that there is nothing wrong with leaving the driver in the bag when the need arises.

3. **Play the hole well.** It's amazing how many golfers forget this when they step up to the first tee shot. It's as though they think that if the tee ball is hot, then the rest will follow naturally. Not true. The first tee shot is just one of several shots you will play on the hole, so you should treat it as you would treat every tee shot, at least on par fours and fives.

Now, what do you see when you stand on a tee? Do you see sand? Trees? Rough? Water hazards? All of these?

This is a classic case of the half-empty way of looking at the glass. You see the trouble, and that's because you're thinking negatively.

It's far smarter to look down the fairway and see your ball flying the way you want to hit it, and landing where you want it to land. Certainly any trouble out there will affect your club selection and the shot you hit, but once you're ready to hit, you should see nothing but the shot. In other words, look at the glass as half full (or even fuller).

Trouble

The key to smart trouble play: Get out of it fast. If that sounds obvious, you wouldn't know it from looking around. Most amateur golfers gamble by trying to hit a high-risk shot that, if pulled off successfully, will result in a miraculous recovery.

The problem is, miracles come few and far between. It is far smarter to take your medicine and get out of trouble by the easiest route. Even Tour pros have to remind themselves of this one. It's not mandated that you have to chip out of trouble, it just makes so much more sense. I'm a pretty aggressive player, and sometimes it irks me to have to chip out, but put it this way: A golfer cannot hit a golf ball through a tree.

This is how simple it is: Let's say you've hit into trees. You're a few yards off the fairway. There is a wide-open escape route that will leave you on the fairway but no closer to the hole. You will, however, have a clear shot at the green.

A more direct route involves hitting between two trees and over another. If you can make it, you will be 150–160 yards closer to the hole, and very close to the green.

If a miracle happens, and you pull of the second option, you may get up and down for par.

If you take the easy route and chip out sideways, you'll probably make bogey.

At this point, bogey is a better score—because if the miracle doesn't happen (and the odds are against you), you will need another miracle just to make bogey. And if now you opt to chip out, then double bogey is your likely score.

This is one of the simplest bits of reasoning you will encounter on a golf course, yet so many golfers either don't get it, or refuse to believe it. Those are the folks who don't play smart golf.

Should you shoot for par on the first hole? If you're a mid- to low-handicapper and the hole is such that par is a reasonable score, then go ahead. But there will be occasions when the hole is tough. It may simply be long, or it may demand a carry over water jutting into the fairway. In such cases, you can still think of par, but you should approach the hole as if it were a par five. Count on reaching the green in three shots, the third being a chip you hope you can get close enough for you to one-putt for your par. And if it doesn't work? Bogey, may not be an ideal way to start off a round, but it's not the worst score you could post.

Another thing to consider before hitting is where to tee the ball up. You would not believe the amount of times I've seen amateurs just walk up to the tee and plant their pegs without thinking of positioning. Some find the nicest, flattest area of grass to tee their balls, without thinking that your feet should get priority on the best ground. They need to control your balance, after all, while the ball will be off the ground.

Beyond that, where you tee the ball depends on the shape of the hole and the shape of your natural shot. Generally, if you hit a draw you should consider hitting from the left of the tee box, and aim down the right of the fairway. The opposite goes for those who fade the ball. There may be instances—dictated by the design of the hole—when you want to favor a different part of the tee.

Advanced players may also want to consider any slope on the tee. A ball teed slightly below the feet should work from left to right, as though you're hitting from a downhill lie. Likewise, a ball teed above the feet should fly naturally from right to left, as though hit from an uphill lie.

How high you tee the ball also depends on a number of things. The optimum position should have about half the ball showing above the driver at address (assuming you've grounded your club). A ball teed lower likely will catch the lower half of the clubface, fly lower and from left to right. A ball teed higher will do the opposite (although clubs and balls are so forgiving today that you seldom see much movement on these shots). A ball teed higher is likely to fly higher, not a bad thing if the wind is behind you and you're looking for distance. Conversely, if the wind is in your face, you may want to tee the ball lower.

On the subject of head wind, something to remember: hitting the ball harder will not give you more distance. It's more likely that the ball will spin more, causing it to rise up in the air, exactly where you don't want it. If you face a strong head wind, make your normal swing and, if anything, concentrate more on your swing action. With a head wind, in other words, it's more important to swing well than to swing hard.

Par threes involve a different set of decisions. You first must determine where you want the ball to come to rest, thinking more specifically than you would on a par four or five. This should be determined by the design of the green, any hazards, and the hole location. You should next consider the weather conditions, in particular the direction and strength of the wind. Check the wind on the tee, up at the hole (what's the flag doing?), and then the wind between tee and green. To do the last, check the *tops* of any nearby trees. Your ball will not spend much time at ground level, so you're checking the conditions it will most likely encounter after you've hit.

Now you're ready to think of club selection, and that will also depend on the type of shot you want to hit— draw, fade, etc.—based on all the information you've gathered and processed. If in doubt, go for the simplest shot and aim for the center of the green. I once read a hilarious story about tour pro Jesper Parnevik, who was playing in a team event with fellow Swede Annika Sorenstam. Jesper really likes to work the ball with his irons (and he's very good at it), but on this occasion, on a par three, he was having trouble picking a club.

At which point Annika suggested, "What's the matter?" Annika asked.

Always Use a Tee!

Some golfers find it really cool to drop a ball on the tee of a par three and hit from the carpet.

Bad idea.

In the first place, the ground on a tee usually is more compacted than on the fairway, so any attempt to replicate an approach from the fairway will be wasted.

More important, however, is the fact that a ball on a tee will not have anything between club and ball at impact. If you catch a ball slightly fat when not using a tee, then some dirt or grass will affect impact. Not a lot, mind you—but why take the slightest chance when you can tee the ball?

"I can't make up my mind whether to hit a soft 6-iron with a bit of cut to it, a low punch with a 7-iron, or a high draw with an 8-iron," Jesper replied.

"Why don't you just hit a straight shot to the middle of the green?"

He didn't know what to say. I guess the lesson is that, even though it's a truism that a pro who hits a straight ball probably made a mistake, it's also true that sometimes you can try to extract too much from a shot. You should consider everything, but not to the point that you're guilty of that old saw, paralysis by analysis.

HOLE STRATEGIES AND COURSE MANAGEMENT

All the work on your swing and all the practice on and around the green will go for nought if you do not manage yourself properly on the golf course.

Actually, this process should begin before you get to the course. Remember how we discussed how smart it is to play a course in your mind before you reach it?

We'll call that preliminary course management. You'll have predetermined where you can go for birdie, where par is a good score, where bogey and double bogey must be avoided at all costs. You'll have put yourself in a frame of mind such that you have a game plan from the beginning.

Management on the course is about putting that game plan into action and sticking to it throughout the round.

GENERAL STRATEGY

No two holes play exactly alike. Some holes may look similar, but chances are their greens are different, they may play in different directions (so the wind has a different effect), or the hazards will be different, and they may need slightly different clubs for the approach. But there are general hole strategies to which a smart golfer adheres.

One approach that applies to all holes is to play it backwards in your mind before playing it forward for real. I've heard it said that you should think two shots ahead, but I'd advise that you think of playing the entire hole. (Of course it helps if you're familiar with the hole; if not, you may have to rely on either a good yardage book or the advice of a wise caddie.)

You do this because the one thing that can be said about playing golf without fear of contradiction is that the ultimate destination for the ball is the hole. The thought process then goes like this:

1. Where on the green do you want to land your ball to give you the best chance of a putt?

2. How much risk will this involve in terms of avoiding hazards or slopes that may kick your ball off the green?

3. If this strategy is too risky, where's the next best place? (Note that uphill putts tend to be easiest, so you ideally want to land your ball below the hole, which, for drainage reasons, usually is at the front of the green. There may be pin positions—cups that are

guarded in front by water, for example—that still carry too much risk.)

On par threes, only the above three questions need be answered.

4. In order to reach your chosen target, what's your best approach shot? Note that if a Tour pro cannot reach a green, or get really close to it, in one shot, he (or she) will lay up to the position that leaves the shortest *full* shot. That way he can put his normal, repetitive, muscle-memorized swing on the ball, and not have to resort to gauging how hard he should swing, or whether he should fly or bump the ball toward its target.

5. In order to reach that position, what's the ideal tee shot or, on par fives, the best second shot? Note that the shortest route to a green isn't always the best approach. It usually is the *clearest* route. You also should shy away from hitting your tee ball into an area that will leave an awkward stance. You can't really do better than a clear shot from a flat lie.

6. Finally, on par fives that you feel you cannot reach (or get close) in two, where do you want to hit your tee shot to give you the easiest second shot? Again, clear and flat works best.

So now you're back on the tee, figuratively speaking, ready to play the hole for real.

Tsk, Tsk

Here are some mistakes that smart golfers do not make. Some I've witnessed personally.

• Not leaving enough time to warm up. Rushing to the first tee is not the ideal way to start a round of golf.

• Trying to lay up close to a hazard. Be safe and back off.

• Muscling a driver on a short par four. They're short enough to play safe.

• Hitting when not ready to hit. I understand that you don't want to slow things down, but more shots overall means more time, too. Stop and start again.

• Putting out after a long lag on a short but not necessarily a gimme putt. Mark and move away.

• Hitting with the wrong club when you *know* it's the wrong club. This usually happens when playing cart golf. So play cart golf. Go back and get the right club.

• Thinking negatively about a tough shot. They say you can talk yourself into hitting a bad shot. They are correct.

• Hitting greenside shots at a tight pin position when the smart thing to do is hit away to the pin to a larger part of the putting surface. The priority is to putt, not necessarily to leave a short putt.

• Trying to hit a perfect long iron that will not reach the green, when two easier iron shots will. The count remains the same.

• Not taking enough club. If you're between clubs, always take the longer one. And don't take anything off it, either.

6

Short-Game Smarts...............................

GREENSIDE, PUTTING, AND SAND

So many golfers waste strokes when they get within 30 yards of the green—and I'm not talking about three-putting. I'm talking about an inability to regularly get into the hole in two strokes.

This shouldn't be the case because, relatively speaking, these are the simplest shots in golf, and the shots on which pros really have little advantage over even high handicappers.

Think about it. I may be able to hit long, straight drives—270 yards and longer—with the consistency that an amateur just can't match. And I can hit middle-iron approaches with much greater accuracy than an amateur. These are full-swing shots that benefit from the technique and the hours of practice that separate the pros from amateurs (and even some other pros).

But the short game? You and I both can hit a golf ball 20 yards. We don't need to employ full swings, either. Arc, swing plane, swing speed—all these things have less importance in the short game. The chip I hit to three feet is a shot you can easily hit.

Yet this is an area that pros and amateurs seem to be farthest apart.

The reason, I think, is that pro golfers realize the importance of the short game to scoring well, and focus more on it. We don't see a short-game shot as an exercise in moving the ball closer to the hole. We see it as getting the ball right next to the hole, and sometimes even in it. Having reached that decision, we know that the only way we can do it is to consider every aspect of the shot. We look at:

- Where the hole is cut
- The contours of the green between the ball and the hole
- The contours of the entire green
- The speed of the green
- The combined effect of speed and contours
- The existence and positioning of hazards, if any
- The territory between the ball and the hole—fairway or rough, or both?
- The weather conditions
- The lie of the ball (very important)
- The status of the match (in match play)

If this seems a lot to consider in playing such a short shot, remember that you'd consider them all on a long shot, and both long and short shots count the same when you add up your score. In fact, the smart golfer has realized this, to the point that he or she considers everything he or she can on every single shot.

You'll also notice that, just as you play a hole backwards in your mind before playing it forward for real, you figure out the short shots by working back from the hole to your ball.

At any rate, once we have fed all this information into the computer, we leave ourselves with three decisions to make:

1. What trajectory of shot should I play? (I'll discuss this in greater detail shortly.)
2. Where do I want the ball to land *first*?
3. Which club should I use to pull off the first two decisions successfully?

Let me come back to number two briefly, since I cannot emphasize enough how important it is. On short shots, pros, with very few exceptions, pick a target spot to aim at. Not a single blade of grass, mind you, but a target small enough and specific enough that missing it will result in a poor shot.

Amateurs don't do this as much as they should. I know of several good amateurs who will do it routinely on, say, a bump and run from 10–15 yards off the green, but I don't know of many who do it on every shot. And that's a shame because, again, pros have no advantage in this area. With a little practice, an 18-handicapper can choose a target just as easily as a pro (the practice is required so it's easier to choose a trajectory; you will learn how the ball reacts when it lands following different trajectories and find it easier to choose a target).

Think about it. Golf places higher significance on— and greater reward for—accuracy the closer you get to the hole. From the tee you are asked to hit an area 15–20 yards wide, double that if your aim is only to hit the fairway as opposed to the right or left of it. The second shot on a par five usually must find an area slightly thinner, and one probably guarded more closely by rough and hazards. The shot to the green must land in an area several yards in diameter. A long putt must ideally come to rest in an area slightly larger than six feet in diameter (within three feet of the hole), while a putt that is holed will have hit a target only 4½ inches wide. In the course of playing a hole, your target area has shrunk to 160th of its original size.

To Lob or Not?

A relatively recent addition to the golf club universe is the third, or "lob," wedge. This is a wedge with about 60 degrees of loft that is used to hit high shots that land softly, usually to a tight pin position. Other occasions when you should consider using a lob wedge include when the green is sloping away from you and is very fast, from a bunker with a high face (they usually come with bounce), when the green is very elevated, and when the hole is close to where you're chipping from (when you have little green to work with, in other words).

Where does the short shot target fit in? Well, it should come to rest in the same area as a long lag putt, because the idea here also is to leave yourself a very makeable putt. But because this shot will bounce and roll, you have another target, which I'll call the primary target. This is the area that you want the ball to hit *first*.

Easier said than done, especially if you don't practice it much. But because it's such a key component of the short game, it's actually something that should be prac-

---

The Belly Wedge

It's always a good idea to use your putter when just off the green (on links courses such as those the British Open visits, you can use it from *way* off the green). But there will be occasions when your ball is sitting in light rough just off the green, too close to the hole for you to comfortably hit a chip, and too far down in the grass for you to make clean contact with your putter.

Answer: the belly wedge.

The idea here is to use a sand wedge and strike the equator of the ball with the leading edge of the club. The shape of the wedge should cut through (or over) the grass. Just be careful that you don't hit below the equator (you're hitting so lightly that the ball will hardly move) or above it (you'll top the ball and leave it in the rough).

This is a shot worth practicing, and most practice greens have longer grass around them.

---

ticed a lot. Fortunately, it can be practiced almost anywhere, because the aim is simply to become a sharpshooter with a number of different clubs. You could chip into a bucket in your own backyard, or you could lay a

Home, Sweet Home

The short game—chipping, pitching, and putting—is an area of the game that needs a lot of practice. It's also the area that's the *easiest* to practice because you don't have to be at a golf course to do it. Translation: It's a smart move to practice your short game at home.

You can do anything from chipping into a plastic bucket in your backyard to putting into a turned-over glass in your living room. You won't replicate exactly the conditions you'd encounter on a golf course, but you will get a good sense of feel.

You can practice your ball position and putting stroke even without using a ball. And simply hitting pitches and chips at any target will give you a better understanding of the relationship between the length of your backswing and the rate of acceleration through impact. That's what feel is all about.

few clubs down to form a square or triangle on a practice green, and chip into that. Whatever you choose, you should practice with as many different clubs, and from as many different lies, as possible. That's because you shouldn't always use the same club for chipping since you're unlikely to see the same chip—same lie, approach conditions, etc.—twice.

The ability to hit the target regularly will improve your short game more than you can imagine. It's true that if you choose the wrong spot, then you're back where you started, but choosing the right spot comes with experience. Studying the situation and environment before you hit, and then studying the result after you hit, will give you enough feedback so that soon the choice of target can be made quickly and wisely.

Before you choose your target area, however, you will choose trajectory. Simply put, a low-running shot is generally preferable to a higher shot, although conditions may indicate otherwise.

You'd never know this were you to conduct a quick survey at a local club. You'd see golfers getting to within spitting distance of a green, then pulling out some fancy lob wedge and trying to airmail the ball to the hole. That may be the shot to play in certain situations, but it should never be the automatic choice since so many things can go wrong. You may make poor contact. You may decelerate and then chunk the shot or leave it way short. You may make too short a backswing, then jerk the club into the ball, which usually results in a good blading and the ball whisking away over the green. You may hit too far—it's a very tough shot on which to gauge distance. A gust of wind may blow your ball off course. It's just not a smart shot to play.

Having said that, there may be circumstances where it's the only shot to play. If there is sand or water between your ball and the green, then you may have to take the aerial route. But note that I said "green" and not "hole," because if there's a route that takes water or sand out of play and still allows you a putt, then the smart thing is to opt for *that* shot.

It's also a good idea to fly the ball to the hole if the flag is cut on the highest of several tiers, or if the grass on which you would normally pitch and run the ball is wet and likely to halt the ball in its tracks.

Whatever shot you choose, the length of the backswing will in large part determine how well you play the shot. All shots should be hit with the clubhead accelerating through impact, although not all at the same rate. A shorter shot will require less acceleration than, say, a shot from 20 yards. Because you will want to maintain good rhythm on your shots, rather than making the mistake of swinging harder on longer shots and more softly on shorter shots, the key to varying the acceleration is to vary the length of the backswing.

This is a part of the short game that can be difficult to master, but it can be done with practice. And as you practice you'll start to get a *feel* for the correct length of backswing and, therefore, the correct rate of acceleration. Just make sure you hit all your shots with the same rhythm.

Here's a question many amateur golfers get wrong: Should you leave the flag in the hole or remove it when chipping? The answer is that you should always leave it in. A lot of golfers may have seen shots during televised tournaments hit the flagstick and stay out, but statistical studies have shown that 33 percent more chips go in the hole when the flag is left in. It's also true that a lot of pros prefer to remove the flag. I've seen Raymond Floyd remove the flag and chip in a couple of times in a single round, but because Raymond can do it doesn't make it a rule of thumb. Raymond has one of the best short games golf has ever seen. If anything, he's the exception to the rule.

PUTTING—THE RUB OF THE GREEN

Good news—you know more about putting than you think you do. In comparison to, say, hitting long irons, there is little technique involved. Put another way, there is little natural ability involved. Once you have mastered a steady stroke (see sidebar "Putting Technique") all that is left is learning how to read greens and putting strategy. And practice, practice, practice.

Putting Technique

This book isn't really about technique, but putting is such a level playing field that a few simple tips should be all that are needed.

1. Keep your head rock steady throughout the putt.

2. Keep your wrists firm but your grip light.

3. When you take your stance, your eyes should be directly over the ball. The ball should be midway between your feet.

4. Imagine a triangle formed by the shoulders, arms, and hands. Swing this triangle like a pendulum.

Reading greens is like preparing for other short shots: You collect as much information, process it in your mind, and then hit the putt based on feel. And feel, as I explained earlier in this chapter, is a result of your learning and becoming comfortable with the relationship between the length of your backswing and the rate of acceleration through the ball. You will have often heard golfers telling a fellow player, "You put a good stroke on it." They are seeing someone who has found his feel.

The process begins, of course, with your reading the green. This begins not once you have reached the green and have marked your ball, but as you approach the

The Big No-No—and I Should Know

Tap-ins are exactly what they should be: Putts so short that you can simply tap the ball into the hole. But sometimes even that can go wrong.

In The Players Championship a few years ago, Lanny Wadkins left a putt on the lip, and stabbed at the back of the ball with the intention of knocking the ball into the hole with a glancing blow. Lanny missed the ball then tapped in conventionally but, because he had intentionally made a stroke, he had to count the miss as well. So he got down into two from two inches. How smart is that?

But as bad as that may have been, it's not unlike the careless mistake I made in the third round of the 1983 British Open.

I faced a six-incher for par on the 14th hole at Royal Birkdale. Leaned over, grounded my club, tried to backhand the tap-in—and whiffed. Missed it completely, and to this day I don't know how it happened. Worse, I finished second to Tom Watson—by a single stroke.

Did it cost me the British Open? Obviously not. It counted no more than any other stroke—and I hit 275 others that week. It's also worth noting that, if I hadn't whiffed the six-incher, I might have been in a playoff, and would not have won outright.

It is just a shining example of how it's a smart idea to focus and concentrate on executing every shot, from the 250-yard drive to the two-inch tap-in.

green and first see its contours. It should be clear if you face a downhill, uphill, or sidehill putt—clear enough for you to start thinking about the speed of your putt. Let me point out here the importance of getting a feel for speed. If you think of rounds you have played in the past, how often did you miss the hole by a lot to the right or to the left? Probably not often, and you are not alone. Most

---

Marking Your Ball

The Rules of Golf do not say exactly *what* you should mark your ball with, but I'd advise either a proper ballmark or a small coin. To mark your ball, lay the mark behind it, then lift and clean your ball (with a cloth, not saliva). To replace it, put the ball down and remove the mark.

If your mark is on someone else's line, move it a putterhead length in a certain direction (pick out a tree or bush, or similar). When it is your turn to putt, make sure that you replace your ball in its original position. If you play it from the position to which you moved it, you will be penalized.

---

golfers get a good read on putts, but misjudge the pace, running the ball too fast, and missing the break, or not hitting the putt hard enough, thereby allowing it to break too much in addition to coming up short. You'll also hear golfers describing a putt as a "speed putt." These usually are fast putts, but I think of *all* putts as speed putts.

Once you reach the green, you should mark your ball (see sidebar "Marking Your Ball") as promptly as possible, taking care not to step on anyone else's line, then prepare to hit your putt—even if you are not away. Reading putts is important, but it should not delay play, so the sooner you start the process, the better.

As well as studying the contours of the green from behind the ball, behind the hole, and from the sides, you should also check for grain—the prevailing direction in which the grass is growing. On Bermuda grass greens, which are prevalent in hotter climates, it can be tough to pick out the grain, principally because Bermuda tends to grow to the southwest, the direction from which the sun

---

Fast and Slow

Greens will be faster:
• Early in the morning, after they have been mowed
• On hot, dry days
• Late in the year (where seasons affect the course) when they have experienced a lot of traffic

Greens will be slower:
• Late in the day
• On wet days
• When the dew has not burned off
• Earlier in the year, before they get a lot of traffic

---

is strongest. But it also can twirl. Bent grass, popular in northern states, is a truer putting surface, because it grows in a consistent direction—toward drainage, which often means downhill. To spot the grain, look for a sheen on the grass. When you can see that, you'll know that the grain is running away from you; putts in that direction will be faster than putts against the grain. Similarly, if you're putting with the grain coming from one side or the other, a putt that breaks with the grain will break faster and more severely than a putt that breaks against the grain. Think of it like swimming with the tide (down-grain) and against it (into the grain).

Another good source of information is what happens to other putts. If you are not away, watch how other players' putts roll—especially if you are going to be hitting on much the same line. I would not, however, advise that you listen to another player who says something like, "Wow! I really hammered that," after coming up short. Apart from the fact that it's against the Rules to dispense advice, he or she may be guilty of a little gamesmanship. Watch the putts and draw your own conclusions.

You also can overread a putt. Usually your first close look at the line of your putt will give you the best sense of what it's going to do. Subsequent reads should confirm this more than contradict it. But if you overanalyze the putt, you may start seeing breaks and rolls that really aren't there. This is especially true with flat putts. I read the final putt of the 1998 U.S. Senior Open at Riviera as dead straight, but I read it over and over simply because I couldn't believe that it would be straight—how often do you have one of those to win a major championship? In fact, it was all I could do to knock it right at the cup. Thankfully, it was the correct read and it fell in.

Before you hit your putt, you should make sure your line to the hole is clear. Ask your playing partners to lift and mark their balls if any are in the general direction of the hole, lift any loose impediments (leaves, and such), and repair any ballmarks (but not spikemarks—that's illegal). The correct way to repair a ballmark is to gently prize the turf back to the surface on all sides, then tap the green flat with your putter. A lot of golfers repair only the turf at the front of the ballmark. But full shots to greens push the turf up at the front when they hit the ground. If you do not repair this, then you may have to putt over an almost imperceptible bump.

Once you have decided on your line, take a few practice strokes while looking at the line. Just as we talked before about visualizing a full shot before you hit it, putts should be handled likewise. Visualize the ball rolling and breaking toward the hole; see it go in and remember the pace.

I said earlier that the perfect putt would roll about 12–18 inches past the hole were it not to go in. Trying to do this ensures that you at least make it to the hole. The old adage "Never up, never in" really is true.

By the same token, if a putt breaks at the hole, make sure it has not broken below the hole before reaching it. It should break on the high side of the hole; what we call the pro side. A putt that has already broken is not likely to turn and roll uphill (although it's been known to happen on Bermuda grass greens). A putt that is breaking in the direction of the hole, on the other hand . . .

When you are ready to pull the trigger, pick out a spot on the line. It could be a few inches from your ball, or it could be several feet; it doesn't matter. But the only time you should not pick a spot is when you face such a long putt that you're hitting to an area around the hole.

The aim is to hit a straight putt over this spot. Let me emphasize *straight*: every putt should be hit with the clubface square to the target line. The speed and contour of the green will take care of break and direction.

In an ideal world, you'll hole everything you hit, but it's not too smart to think that way. Unless you are within makeable range—10–20 feet—you should try to get the ball to tap-in range. If the putt falls, that's a bonus. Beyond that, the idea is to lag the putt to within three feet of the hole. If you've been practicing your putting as much as you should, anything within three feet should be simple.

In the event that you do hit past the hole, do not look

away until your ball stops rolling. Instead, watch closely what your putt does *past* the hole, for this will provide valuable information for your comeback putt.

When you're done, get out of your fellow golfers' way, and keep still. When play has finished, you may want to check for other damage to the green—spike-marks, other ballmarks—and repair it. It is legal after you've putted. But do not delay play.

SAND SMARTS

The main thing to do to improve your sand play is to practice your technique so it becomes the last thing you have to think about.

If your technique is good, you then can concentrate on where to hit behind the ball, how much to open the clubface, which club to use, where to aim for.

That said, here are a few smart tips:

- Don't assume you have to hit toward the hole. Your first priority is to get out of the bunker. If the lip between your ball and the hole is too high, or if you're so close to the front wall that you don't think you can get the ball out, aim in a different direction, making sure that you can now get out, and that you can play from the area you've chosen to hit to.

- Your second priority is to get down in one putt, or two at the most. In the Introduction to this book, I talk about hitting away from the hole to assure I'd score bogey instead of gambling and possibly—make that probably—coming away with double bogey or worse. That's smart thinking.

- Don't assume you have to use a sand wedge. A pitching wedge can work in firm, wet sand. A 9-iron is a good club to use when your ball is buried (don't worry about identifying it first; there's no penalty for playing the wrong ball in a hazard). And if you have to hit over a low lip to a tight pin, a putter has been known to work.

- Don't ground your club in sand. It's a hazard. Grounding the club will cost you two penalty strokes.

- Remove anything man-made—(cigarette butts, bottle-tops, etc.)—but do not touch anything natural (stones, twigs, leaves, etc.).

- You can take your golf bag and clubs into sand and even put them down—just so long as you do not test the texture of the sand with them.

- Shrug your shoulders and waggle the club as you address the ball. It's crucial that you get rid of tension.

- A ball hit from wet sand will spin less than a ball hit from soft, fluffy sand. Aim shorter and let it roll.

- On long sand shots, eliminate lower-body action and make sure you hit the ball first. "Getting out is first priority" still applies.

7

Using the Rules.................................

A thorough knowledge of the Rules of Golf not only prevents you from needlessly throwing away strokes by inadvertently breaking a rule, but it also allows you to follow procedures that work to your advantage.

An example: Let's say that you have hit into a lateral water hazard (marked by red lines or stakes). A smart golfer knows his options. He can replay the shot. He can drop his ball within two clublengths of where his ball last crossed the margin of the hazard. Or he can drop his ball on either side of the hazard (he would not have this last option with a water hazard, marked by yellow lines or stakes).

Let's say he chooses option two. Once he drops he will have a clear shot to the green, and not a terribly difficult one—were it not for the fact that the ground where he has to drop is really uneven. His ball has a very good chance of rolling into a hole—if for no other reason than gravity. Then he notices an area where he is entitled to drop that slopes drastically toward the hazard. The smart golfer can make this work to his advantage. He knows that if his ball, after being dropped, rolls into a hazard, closer to the hole, or more than two clublengths from where it hit the ground, he is entitled to redrop. And if it does either of these things a second time, then he must *place* his ball where it hit the ground on the second drop—possibly getting a lie that will allow him to hit the shot to the green. In stroke play, this could save a valuable stroke. In match play, it could make the difference between losing a hole and winning it.

The Rules of Golf are full of such options, situations in which you can use the Rules to your advantage without actually breaking them—or even bending them significantly. An example of the latter would involve a player who found his shot blocked but came up with a novel way of getting relief. Just beyond his ball was a cart path. The Rules allow a free drop if the cart path interferes with your ball, stance, or swing. The player knew that his nearest point of relief would give him a clear shot, so he called over a Rules official and told him the path was interfering with his stance.

The official was puzzled. It was beyond his ball, he told the player. When he addressed the ball, neither he nor the ball was on the path.

"But what if I intend to hit the shot left-handed," the player asked.

"Not only are you right-handed," the official replied, "but if you did that you would be going in the wrong direction."

Well, the player pointed out that sometimes you had

to play left-handed, which is true, and that there is nothing in the Rules that says you have to play right-handed
or left-handed. Nor, for that matter, was there anything in
the Rules that said a player had to take the most direct
route to the hole. He got his relief. This has since been
outlawed, as it should have been, because it is going too
far.

On the other hand, you can use the Rules to your
advantage in the following situations:

• **When your ball comes to rest against a hazard stake.**
  Not many golfers know it, but if the stake is yellow
  (water hazard) or red (lateral water hazard), you may
  remove it before hitting. If it is white (out of bounds),
  you may not.

  And remember to mark your ball and lift it before
  removing the stake. If you don't and your ball moves
  in the removal process, you will suffer a penalty
  stroke.

• **When you are entitled to clean your ball.** A clean ball
  is always better to play with than a dirty one, so
  learn the situations in which you are entitled to clean.
  You can clean your ball:

  • when you are on the green
  • when you declare a ball unplayable
  • when you are allowed free relief, from, for
    example, an immovable obstruction, casual water,
    or ground under repair
  • when your ball is embedded
  • when you cannot identify a ball as yours. Note in
    this instance that you must clean only enough of

your ball to identify it, and that you may not clean it to identify it in a hazard, for there is no penalty for hitting the wrong ball from a hazard.

- **When you hit your tee shot on a par three into a water hazard.** You may have an option to drop, with a penalty stroke, closer to the hole than one tee is, but you won't get a better lie than on a tee or a better stance than in the teeing area. In this situation, take the option of replaying the shot.

- **When you are between holes.** Let's say your putting is not up to snuff. The Rules ban practice during a round, except when that practice involves putting and chipping. You are entitled to putt or chip on the green of the hole you played last, on a practice green, or on the tee of the hole you are about to play. Just don't hold up play.

- **When you are about to play a match.** The Rules do not allow you to practice on a competition course any time on the same day of a stroke-play competition, but they do allow you to practice on it before a match-play competition.

- **When you are about to take relief.** If you have chosen the option of dropping your ball, you are allowed to clear the area of any loose impediments (but you cannot repair pitchmarks and the like). It's true that you remove loose impediments—natural objects, such as sticks and stones—at any time, except when you are in a hazard. The advantage here is knowing you can do this *before* you drop. Now you

remove the risk of making your ball move
as you remove them, a transgression that carries a
penalty.

- **When your ball overhangs the hole.** Many golfers
believe that when the ball overhangs the hole, the
player must go up to it and tap it in. Not so. It's
true that a rule was enacted in the mid-1980s to
prevent players from waiting an eternity for a puff
of wind to blow in an overhanging ball. Now a
player must walk to his ball and *after 10 seconds*,
must deem his ball at rest and tap it in (if not he is
deemed to have holed it with his last shot and adds
a penalty stroke). Many golfers forget the 10-
second part of the rule, and 10 seconds can be a
pretty long wait.

- **When it's windy.** This isn't really using the Rules to
your advantage as much as understanding the
Rules. When the wind gets up and you stand over
a putt, if the ball moves before you hit it, and you
have addressed the ball—which is to say you have
grounded the club and have taken your stance—
then you are deemed to have moved it and you
must add a penalty stroke. This can happen
anywhere on the course, but is most likely to
happen on the putting green, where there is the
least grass resistance. Therefore, you should not
address the ball before you putt. And before you
start scratching your head and wondering how you
can putt without addressing your ball, remember
that the definition of addressing the ball requires

that you take your stance and ground your club. Windy weather solution? Take your stance but *do not ground the club*. Hover it just above the putting surface, directly behind the ball.

- **When an opponent's ball is in your way.** Note I didn't say "on your line." That's obvious, and refers to the putting green. But you can ask another player to mark his ball *anywhere* on the course. The situations in which you would require another player to mark when he is not on the green are limited, but do exist. Let's say, for example, that you want to bump and run the ball to the hole. If the other player's ball is within your target area (and remember, I advocate *always* choosing a target area for a greenside shot), then you should have him mark it and remove the risk of your hitting his ball. Were you to hit his ball, your opponent would have to replace the ball, but yours likely would bounce off in a direction you certainly didn't intend when you hit the shot.

- **When you can't see the putting surface.** This normally would be considered a blind shot, but it doesn't have to be totally blind. If you have a chip or pitch to a putting surface well above your lie, and you can't see the flag—never mind the hole— then you can request that a caddie, or another golfer, hold up the flag to indicate your line. Under the Rules, he would be tending it. Once again, you're removing the guesswork.

In fact, a lot of using the Rules of Golf to your advantage involves removing the guesswork. After all, if you are completely conversant with the Rules and how they can affect various situations, what is there to guess?

Let the other guys make mistakes.

8

Anatomy of a
Smart Round....................

In chapter 5 we talked about preparing to play. Now we're going to take a look at how to think and play your way around a golf course. A *real* golf course.

It would be easy for me to cover the general methods of playing par threes, fours, and fives. Always hit the fairway, keep your ball below the hole on approach shots, don't try to hit to holes that are closely guarded by trouble when there is significant putting acreage a little farther from the hole. The obvious stuff. And we already have discussed how the smart way to play any hole is to think backwards from the hole itself: where you want to putt from, where you'd best hit your approach from to reach the spot you feel you should putt from, and so on.

But I think you'd learn as much if not more if I take you through an actual round of golf, one in which good smart play was absolutely crucial—not a casual round in other words, not even close to casual. I'll describe my approach to each hole and how I actually played it, and touch on some of the do's and don'ts that can be learned by amateur golfers who might find themselves in similar situations.

The round I've chosen is the fourth round of the 1998 U.S. Senior Open at Riviera Country Club in Pacific Palisades, Calif. I've chosen it for several reasons. One is that it was the round that won me the championship. I'd started off, after all, with a 77 and, having hoisted myself into contention during rounds two and three, with a 68 followed by a 71, it was essential that I played smart golf in the final round.

I also have chosen it because many golfers are to some extent familiar with the Riviera layout. It has been the frequent site of the Los Angeles Open since 1926, it held the U.S. Open in 1948 (Ben Hogan won), and has twice held the PGA Championship—in 1983, when Hal Sutton won and first was dubbed "The Next Nicklaus," and in 1995 when Steve Elkington won his first major championship. As most of those events were televised, a lot of golfers may have seen at least the back nine on television. Hopefully, you'll be able to relate directly to my own situation.

Last, Riviera has a tremendously good mix of holes, long and short par threes (and even a par three with a bunker in the middle of the green!), a tiny par four and a par five that is unreachable in two (not a common hole in courses the pros play). Riviera also has tough kikuyu rough, which places an even greater emphasis on precision. In other words, I'll be able to discuss a variety of ways to play the game. As I often have said, there are lots of ways to play golf; you just have to find the one that suits you best. Let's go.

No. 1, 501-Yard Par Five

Professional golfers automatically think birdie on a par five. We can't afford not to because, with such a high level of talent and such sophisticated equipment, most par fives are reachable in two. For all other golfers but skilled amateurs, on the other hand, par fives are the *last* place they should be thinking birdie, because the farther the hole is from the tee, the more opportunities there are, so to speak, to hit bad shots. The best thing an amateur can think on the tee of a par five is "What are my true expectations?" but certainly not "What are my hopeful expectations?" He (or she) must dissect the hole into thirds or fourths or fifths, however many shots it will reasonably take to the green, and then hit to those areas.

This hole was especially significant at the Senior Open because it was important for me to get off to a good start, to establish a good foundation. It's not a particularly difficult hole, because the elevated tee shortens it, but I still had to be careful. My aim was to hit the fairway, avoiding not only the rough but out of bounds left and heavy trees to the right. I also wanted to hit the fairway (which looked much thinner from the high tee) because hitting from that kikuyu rough would bring a barranca—a run-off drainage ditch—that cut across the fairway about 320 yards out, and I wouldn't get to the green, or close to it, in two.

The barranca is a good example of frontal hazards being real obstacles for amateurs. You'll see a lot of average golfers fretting over water or OB or woods off to the right or left, but the truth is that lateral hazards are not critical to average players unless they're suffering from a severe hook or slice. But to those who hit it straight, and especially to those who don't hit it particularly long, frontal hazards are nothing but trouble.

I began with a good drive, finding the fairway. Now I could go for the green—but not the hole. Not only was the flag tucked behind the front-right bunker, but the putting surface was firm and anything that cleared the bunker probably would not hold the green. I chose to play to the left side, and hit 3-iron. I pulled it a bit, into the rough, but I wasn't too bothered. Because I'd missed it on the side of the green farthest from the hole, I was able to put a swing on the ball, and hit a more predictable shot. I got up and down for the birdie.

There are two smart lessons here. First, it's vital you hit the fairway when you face a long second shot and, second, if you're playing a difficult approach, "miss it" in a position that gives you the best option on your next shot. The latter is why you'll see tour pros happily hit into a front bunker if they don't think they can hit the green. We practice and play sand shots so much that we're confident that we can get up and down. Front bunkers often leave uphill shots.

No. 2, 460-Yard Par Four

This is a tough par four, so tough in fact that I sort of look at the par-five first hole at Riviera as a par four and this par four as a par five (they're both fives for member play). Again, a good drive is ultra important because the second shot is so long. And because this usually is a par five, the green is small, receptive to short irons, and no more than 12 or 15 yards across. In fact, were an amateur to play this sort of hole, the best plan would be to consider it a par five, try to hit the green in three, and take the bogey and run.

After hitting the fairway, I sized up my second shot and figured it was okay to miss the green short, but that anything left or right would have to deal with bunkers or a steep hill. As noted on the first hole, when you face a really tough approach, you have to figure there's a good chance you'll miss the target. You just have to work out the safest miss. Happily, I hit to the fringe and after two putts had a four.

No. 3, 434-Yard Par Four

There's a bunker about 215 yards out on the left-hand side of this slight dogleg-right. There's quite a lot of room to the right—but here we have a good example of how a hole can be set up to sucker you. Next to that room to the right is a heavy stretch of kikuyu grass. Further, the angle into the green is virtually impossible—right over a green-side bunker to a part of the putting surface that runs away from you. So here we have an example of the shortest route to the green turning out to be the route fraught with the most problems. It's far smarter to flirt with the bunker to the left than the rough to the right. As it turned out, I missed the fairway and, because of that, I missed the green. But I got up and down for par and was happy with the four.

No. 4, 238-Yard Par Three

This is a long par three with a wide-yet-shallow green. It's tough to hold, so the smart play is to take the line that follows the fairway up to the right of a bunch of big front bunkers, and try to catch the right of the green. When we play the Los Angeles Open here in winter, there usually is a wind from the ocean blowing up the valley the course sits in, making the hole play even longer. Some years I've hit driver—and how often do you hear of a tour pro hitting driver on a par three?

The long par three is a classic example of a hole on which an amateur should ignore the obvious challenge—to try to hit over the bunkers. It makes much more sense to think of it as a short par four. Hit safely away from the bunkers, then hit a pitch and run, maybe even putter from off-green if the grass is mown closely enough. If you get up and down, you'll have your par—as it turned out, that's what I did—and even if you make four, you shouldn't be concerned, because you definitely will not be the only golfer to score bogey.

No. 5, 426-Yard Par Four

At this point, Raymond Floyd, who'd begun the day three strokes ahead of me, was beginning to struggle; he clearly wasn't on his game. But as I told myself this I immediately stopped the thought process. I had no control over what Raymond was doing, and if I was thinking about his game then I was neglecting my own. From the start of the second round, my game plan had been to dismiss the other players from my mind and concern myself only with playing holes. This was no time to lose focus.

The fifth at Riviera is another long par four but, if you're smart enough, you can shorten it. It's a two-level hole. At the farthest part of the landing area for the drive, the fairway drops down a 25- to 30-foot embankment. If you can catch it you leave a shorter second shot, as well as a better angle into the green—not because of any hazards but because of the angle the green sits at. I'd be hitting into the slope, which would help stop the ball. This is a case of the golfer using the contours of the fairway to his advantage. As a general rule, I always try to hit my drives to run *with* the fairway and leave an approach that will be hit *into* the slope of green.

You also want to drive into a position that leaves you the largest target. A good example of how you can do this is the first hole at the Old Course in St. Andrews, Scotland. It looks fairly innocuous, with a fairway so wide it accommodates the 18th hole coming in the opposite direction. It seems you couldn't hit a bad tee shot short of whiffing or slicing out of bounds, but the truth is that the best drive is hit out to the left, away from the hole, because the best approach is hit from the left. From head-on, the green seems a small target sitting immediately beyond the Swilcan Burn, but from the left, it's a much larger target. In effect, a good drive to the left changes the shape of the green, and you always want to do that if it gives you an advantage.

Back at Riviera, I scored my fourth par in a row, hitting the fairway, hitting the green, and two-putting.

No. 6, 170-Yard Par Three

Length is not the issue here. This is a rare case of a green with a bunker in the middle of it. Come to think of it, it's about the only par three anywhere that has a bunker in the middle of it. It's an interesting hole, and tough—but not as tough as it used to be; the bunker is much shallower than in years past.

I hit 6-iron to 10 feet but missed the birdie putt. I could have looked on that as an opportunity lost, but the greens at Riviera are relatively new, having been redone after the 1996 PGA Championship. So I knew that they hadn't settled into a true roll. That doesn't mean I didn't try to make birdie putts—we think birdie on every hole—it just means that it's better to understand a situation and move on than succumb to frustration.

No. 7, 406-Yard Par Four

This is another position hole. In years past there was out of bounds along the right of this dogleg-right but now it's marked as a lateral hazard. Either way, it complicates matters because the fairway runs away from you and drops off to the left, and the farther left you hit, the more awkward your second shot. The chances are that the ball will be above your feet, which makes the shot a little less predictable. Ideally you want to land on a flat area on the right side of the fairway, but that brings the hazard very much into play.

There's a lesson to learn here. What's smarter—avoiding the hazard at all costs or flirting with it to avoid an uneven lie? Sad to say, there is no clear answer, because it depends on your own game and how well you know it. But if I'm playing well, I'll take my chances with the hazard. I dearly want to hit from an even lie, because the last thing I want is to get stuck in the kikuyu rough around the green.

As it happened, I chose the middle ground, and aimed at the slope. I was figuring that if I aimed at it I wouldn't hit it—and wouldn't you know it: I hit right on the slope, ran left, and gave myself an awkward 7-iron approach. I just choked down, made a little flatter swing, and knocked the ball to within a foot of the hole. That was a big shot, because the tap-in birdie got me into a tie for the lead.

No. 8, 368-Yard Par Four

This hole begins with a very tight tee shot from a chute of trees to a landing area that was much wider in years gone by. There's a fairway bunker about 220 out on the left. I use it as a target and try to fade my ball past it with a 3-wood or driver. This is not a shot I'd advise amateurs to play. It makes much more sense on a hole of this length to lay up and leave a longer approach. It still will only be a middle iron. I drove into the fairway, knocked the approach to about 12 feet, but missed the putt.

No. 9, 418-yYard Par Four

Because the second shot is played uphill, this hole plays longer than its yardage. You always should be aware of what elevation can do to a hole. It doesn't matter whether you're hitting a tee shot or a tiny pitch shot— a change in elevation should always change your thinking. Of course, it's just one part of the computation. You should check out the surrounding environment to get as much information as you can regarding elevation, wind, and even light and shadow. For example, if you're playing on a cold day and there's an area in shadow, chances are if there's been any frost that area will be firmer because it won't have had time to thaw out. That sort of thinking can save you strokes.

There's a bunker to the right of fairway a short distance out, but it doesn't really come into play. What *does* is another bunker, to the left, about 230–240 yards out. If you hit it in there you have no chance of hitting to the green. I avoided it, hit to the green, then missed another 12-footer. At this point I had every reason to view those last two birdie putts as missed opportunities, but it would not have done me any good to dwell on them, so I figured I'd just keep plugging away.

No. 10, 311-Yard Par Four

You read that correctly. A 311-yard par four, one of the shortest par fours we play all year, and living, breathing proof that par fours do not need to be long to be tough. They just have to get your mind working overtime.

The green is driveable by the longest hitters, but it's also extremely narrow, sits at an awkward angle, and has sand wrapping around it. A bunker cuts two-thirds of the way across the right side of the fairway, about 200 yards out. The best tee shot is to lay up beyond the bunker and to the left, and open up the green for the approach. Again, you're thinking backwards from the hole. Were you to stand by the flag and say, "Okay, where's the best place to hit from to get here?" I doubt very much if the answer would be "The tee. Just blast one." You would look for an area of fairway from which you'd encounter the least amount of trouble, one which also is easily reachable from the tee. It's that simple.

And here's what happened. I hit a good tee shot and was left with a wedge. Naturally I'm thinking birdie. The flag was cut at the back of the green, close to the sand. First Raymond hits into bunker. Then I made the classic error of getting too cute and hitting where I shouldn't. I put my shot in the sand as well! Went from thinking birdie to making bogey. First of the day.

So let this be a lesson: Don't assume that a short par four is going to be an easy hole. If anything assume exactly the opposite, and really think about how you plan to play it. If the person who built the hole was worth his salt, he'll have hidden away all manner of problems. Designers, after all, like to play mind games with golfers, and short par fours tend to be where they play most of their favorite tricks.

No. 11, 561-Yard Par Five

The barranca that crosses the first hole also crosses the 11th, only it's a bit farther out from the tee. This is a good example of a feature that does not come into play from the teeing area but nevertheless dictates the tee shot. My aim was to make sure I was past the barranca in two shots; otherwise, I would have a third shot longer than 200 yards—not the smart way to play a par five. And in order to get over in two I had to drive safely.

A bad start. I hit the ball well left, into trees, and after that I had to play out short of the barranca. I had 210 yards for my third shot, and chose a 4-wood. From just off the putting surface I got up and down. With a bogey on a short par four and a par on a hole that should have been birdied, I'd lost two golden chances to go ahead. However, Raymond had done likewise so I hadn't lost any ground.

No. 12, 413-Yard Par Four

We swing around and play in the opposite direction, which means back comes the barranca. This time it's in front of the green, and again it puts demands on your drive, because now if I get into trouble it's in my lay-up area. Fortunately, this is a good driving hole for me since a large tree and a bunker, which normally would make the drive more difficult, actually make it easier. They define the hole and give me a definite target. It's like kicking a ball through goalposts. I hit a drive and a nice 6-iron to about seven feet, but missed the putt.

No. 13, 420-Yard Par Four

The idea on this dogleg-left is to hit a slight draw, catch the contour of the fairway, and propel the ball a little farther. At least that's what you're *supposed* to do. I hit into right rough and had to hack the ball out to about 60–70 yards short of the green. At any rate, I was on in three but missed the par putt and dropped a shot. I was back to even par, but not too surprised because this hole has been a problem for me in the past. Maybe that thought had been lurking in my mind. Or maybe I'd momentarily lapsed into thinking that the Senior Open had come down to Raymond and me—until I looked at the scoreboard and realized Vicente Fernandez had made a bit of a move. Back to reality.

No. 14, 180-Yard Par Three

The green presents a very wide target but not a very deep one, which means you have to think extra hard about club selection and the sort of shot you're going to hit. On holes with shallow greens you should try to hit a higher shot to the green, because it's more likely to land softly and hold. A low shot will scoot right through. Both Raymond and I hit what we thought were pretty good shots—high, into the breeze—but both ended up long. Probably that was because the green was pretty firm. In this case you view it as a rub of the green or, to be more specific, a bounce of the green. We both made par.

No. 15, 447-Yard Par Four

Things are just not getting any easier. The idea here is to clear the crook of the dogleg right, then try to keep the approach shot out of a relatively deep valley in the middle of the green. It's one of those holes on which there aren't really a lot of options.

The ideal tee shot, of course, is a fade. Like most pros, I can play that shot; I can work the ball in different directions. Not too many amateurs can do that, however. So if a hole calls for a fade and your natural shot is a draw, you should work out how to play the hole with a draw, even if it means playing for bogey instead of par. If you don't, and you try to hit a shot you're not capable of hitting, then you will end up in trouble and that could cost you more than a stroke.

I hit a good drive, and left my second shot about 30 feet left of the pin. Raymond hit to about eight feet behind it. I putted once then tapped in. Raymond narrowly missed his putt for birdie. I could see on the scoreboard that Vicente had taken the lead. So this was the situation. At two over par, Vicente led me by one and Raymond by two. If Vicente posted that score, and I think he was on the final hole, then I would have to birdie one of the last three holes to tie him and Raymond would have to birdie two of the last three.

Trouble was, there were no birdie holes left.

No. 16, 168-Yard Par Three

Maybe this hole is birdie-able on some days but *not* on Sunday of the Senior Open. The flag was cut front-left and the green was really firm, which meant the only shot that could get close was one that landed between the kikuyu rough at the front of the green and the hole itself—a three-foot target, in other words.

The green also is almost completely surrounded by sand, but I wasn't too worried about it. I just wanted to leave myself a putt—any putt.

We both hit 6-iron to about 25 feet, our balls coming to rest within a foot of each other. Raymond was away.

As I looked at the putts, I remembered that I'd seen this putt several times before, in several Los Angeles Opens, and I recalled that it almost always broke more than it appeared it would. The only question was whether it *still* would break more, because of the rebuilding of the greens. When Raymond missed his putt, however, he gave me a good read, and I knew it would break just as I thought. From 25 feet, I rolled it in.

The lesson here is that the smart golfer gets to know his golf course and *trusts his instincts*—because often those gut instincts tell you more than your eyes do.

So now I was tied with Vicente. I knew he was on the last hole, so I listened. Didn't hear any roar, so it was safe to assume he'd parred it. We were even.

No. 17, 575-Yard Par Fve

This hole is unreachable in two, so the plan is to leave a short enough third shot. The only way to do that is to hit good first and second shots. If the first goes into the rough, birdie is almost impossible. If the second goes into the rough, you could be close enough to get to the green, but it will be almost impossible to hit and hold and get the ball close. This was, realistically, my only birdie opportunity, because I knew I wouldn't be hitting a short iron to the green on the last hole. I had to hit good first and second shots.

I drove the ball safely. Decision time. Rather than risk hitting a 3-wood to get it well into the scoring area, and leave a sand wedge, I opted for a 2-iron to make sure it stayed in play. It worked. Now I was looking at pitching wedge or 9-iron. The hole was cut on the upper level of the two-tier green. The ideal shot was to hit it into the slope between the tiers, let the slope kill the ball's momentum, and let the ball trickle up to the hole. If I chose the wedge I would have to hit it full, and wasn't too comfortable with the idea. It's a truism on Tour that, if you can't reach a green, you should leave a full wedge shot (as opposed to a half swing), but under the gun these shots can get away from you. I decided instead to hit a little 9-iron, and it came off almost as planned. The slope killed it, but the ball released and rolled to about 15 feet from the hole.

I put what looked like a perfect roll on it, and was sure it was going in. To this day I'll never know how it stayed out. So I parred. Not a bad score for the hole.

Except to win the Senior Open I now had to birdie one of the toughest holes in golf.

No. 18, 447-Yard Par Four

The final hole at Riviera rises up and over a large rise—the landing area is therefore blind—then turns slightly to the right, with the left side of the fairway sloping much more severely than the right. It then sort of moves to the left, to a green nestled back into the side of a hill. When we play the Los Angeles Open here in winter, when the kikuyu grass is dormant, it's not uncommon for a drive that finds the center of the fairway to kick to the right and run down into the right rough, even into trees. But conditions were different in the Senior Open. It was summer and the kikuyu grass was thick, almost blossoming. That meant a "Los Angeles Open drive," started well to the left, might hang up on the hillside, and leave a perilous hanging lie—not the sort of position you want to hit from when you have to make birdie. In addition, the flag was cut back-left, behind a bank of rough cutting into the green from the left. From the top of the fairway, that position was almost unreachable—you'd have to hit a right-to-left shot from a serious left-to-right lie. The ideal approach was therefore from the right side of the fairway. I figured I could start the ball off in the middle, fade it a little, and then let it run with the slope a little without running into trouble—a "Senior Open drive."

It came off perfectly. But now I had another decision to make: go for the flag with a 4-iron and risk ending up in either the bank of rough on the left or the rough behind, or go for the fat part of the green with a 5-iron and try to make a long birdie putt? The risk of finding the rough was tremendous. When I'd been on the practice putting green earlier in the day, I'd watched John Jacobs and Graham Marsh hit into the kikuyu rough, and neither had been able to get the ball even *onto* the putting surface. The recovery is just such a delicate shot that you can't really put a full swing on the ball (as I'd done on the first hole).

Thing is, my playing personality is actually more aggressive than some people think it is. I like to play what I call "aggressively intelligent." The 4-iron was a shot I *knew* I could play. I'd hit it before and I'd hit it well before. I'd also hit it poorly before, but that's not the way to think. The thought pattern is: I have hit it well before.

And the 5-iron was not without its risks, either; it wasn't as if I was *guaranteed* to hit the green.

But what it came down to was this: When you play not to lose, you tend not to win.

I went through my swing thoughts. Don't hit it hard. Hit it high. Keep your left shoulder up (that stops me from pulling the ball). Keep your eye on the ball. Swing within yourself. Fundamental stuff that works for all golfers. Then I swung.

Twelve feet from the hole! I looked at my putt. At first it looked straight, but how could it be? Whoever heard of a straight putt to win a national championship? And at Riviera? So I started looking for some break. Couldn't find any. Remember what we said on the 16th hole, to trust your instincts? As long as I looked, my gut still said "straight." So it was just a matter of getting it rolling.

And in it went. Man, that opening 77 seemed like a lifetime ago.

9

Smart Tournament Golf......................................

PLAYING TOURNAMENT GOLF

At some point you should put your game (and yourself) to the test by playing in a tournament. It's one thing to put in hard work to lower your scores and find out in casual play how low you can go. It's another thing to play in a tournament when your performance is measured not only against your own previous performances but against other players' performances, too. If major championships are the true measure of how good professional golfers can be, then tournament play is the true measure of how good amateurs can be. This does not necessarily include the U.S. Amateur Championship—that probably is not too realistic for most amateurs—but certainly club, local, and regional tournaments. Success in those would bring the amateur into the picture.

There is no hard-and-fast rule about how to play in a tournament; every golfer has his or her own approach. Here's mine (although it is by no means exclusively mine):

One shot at a time.

As much as I may be aware of a particularly difficult hole, or a rough stretch, I can control only the matter at hand, the shot I am about to hit. It's true that I may be setting up a particular shot. For example, if I know I want to hit a putt from below the hole, which I normally do, then I will play proper shots in a way that will lead to the uphill putt. So in that sense I am thinking about a shot down the road. But that's planning as opposed to executing. When I execute I think of only one shot.

That may seem a conservative approach, but it works. Have you noticed how many football coaches or baseball managers talk about taking things one game at a time? It sounds clichéd after a while because they all say it. Or at least all the ones who are around for the long haul say it. That's because it doesn't matter what your sport, when you focus on one shot at a time or one game at a time, or even one pitch at a time, success is usually not too far away. Have you also noticed that coaches or managers who make bold predictions or who have wildly exotic game plans tend not to be around for the long haul?

Some people would call this grinding, a term that usually is used in a derogatory fashion when talking about a player. An example of a player who often was described as a grinder was Curtis Strange. There wasn't much flashy about Curtis's game. He wasn't a power hitter, he wasn't known as an outstanding putter. He just had a solid, all-round game and a tremendous ability to focus on each shot. He just happened to grind his way to back-to-back U.S. Open titles in 1988 and 1989, in the process becoming the first player to win two U.S. Opens in a row since Ben Hogan—who was the game's ultimate grinder.

Who else? . . . Jack Nicklaus. Ground his way to 18 professional majors. Larry Nelson. A U.S. Open and two PGA Championships. Do you notice something? Some of the greatest players to have played the game fit the mold of grinder. Maybe it's a mistake to use the term demeaningly. True, it's not the only way to be successful—I doubt if Arnold Palmer could be described as a grinder, for example, nor Seve Ballesteros—but over the years it's proven to be a very smart approach to playing what can be a very demanding sport.

Grinding works. Look what happened at Riviera in the 1998 U.S. Senior Open. After starting with a 77, as ugly a round of golf as I've played, I realized I had lost my focus. It was time to bear down. One shot at a time. Focus and execute. Let the rest of the field play their own games. What happens, happens. Well, it happened that when I holed that birdie putt on the final green, it was the first time all week that I'd had the lead. The hard work of the final three rounds could not have taken any longer in paying off, but it certainly did.

Another example from about the same time: Lee Janzen in the U.S. Open at Olympic. If ever there is a time and place for grinding to pay off it's on a U.S. Open course once the United States Golf Association has set it up for the national championship. Tall rough, tight fairways, lightning-fast greens. If you stand over your ball and focus on anything other than the shot at hand, you're dead. Lee explained after he won at Olympic, having started the day several shots behind Payne Stewart, that he had decided to think about nothing but each shot as it came up. He had a game plan for each hole and, once he prepared to hit the shot, that was all he thought about. He didn't care whether he finished first or 40th—he'd take the same approach.

He also explained later that between shots he would take a look at the leaderboards, but once he realized with about five or six holes to play that he was in the thick of things, he decided that checking the scoreboards might soften his focus. So he ignored them, too. It wasn't until he had returned a 68 and had checked and signed his scorecard—two under par on the final day of the U.S. Open is just outstanding—that he realized he was about to win. You should take the same approach when you play in your tournaments.

All the material we've gone over in previous chapters should be brought to bear in your tournament preparation and play. You should practice proper diet and nutrition, practice properly, make sure you have the right equipment and the best club makeup for any given day. You also should check the weather forecast.

Those are all smart golf management practices. Smart course management will begin with your familiarizing yourself with the course you are about to play (assuming it's not your home course, which you should know pretty well). It's not always possible to get access to a course for a practice round, particularly if it's a private club (although it never hurts to call and find out). If this is the case, then at least get in contact with the club professional and pick his or her brains. Go over the course hole by hole, and if the professional is too busy to discuss the course, try to arrange a time when you can call back. Even better, arrange a time when you can stop by the pro shop. Even the toniest clubs tend not to stop visitors. The advantage of this is that you can go over the scorecard with the pro, and make notes.

If you do have access to the course, use your practice round wisely. You likely will not have the luxury of hitting several balls. You may, however, be able to hit a few extra putts if the group behind you is not in position to play. Getting to know the greens on a strange course can give you a tremendous advantage in that almost half the shots in a single round are hit on the green.

As discussed before, play each hole backwards in your mind. You may not be able to do this on the tee, but as you approach each green you should be able to get a feel for where the proper landing areas are for tee shots. Let's say for example that you hit your driver, and leave a short-iron approach but from a downhill lie. You should be able to see that as you approach your ball. If so, look around you for a flat area that will not require too great a difference in club selection. Then work out from your yardage book—or eyeball it if you have to—what club would find the flatter area from the tee. Make a note of how you think it best to play the hole on your scorecard. Now, you may already have done this during a conversation with the club professional. If so, double-check what you've been told. If it fits with your own game, go with it. If not, change the game plan and replace the pro's advice with your own decisions. You may want to consider playing a hole the way the pro advises, even if it doesn't fit with your first impression, but ultimately your own instincts should win out.

Another useful plan if you can't get on a course is to try and replicate the course on your home course. For instance, if you know that the course you're about to play has several long par fours, you also know that in all likelihood you'll have to hit several long irons (or even fairway woods) for approach shots. In addition to practicing these shots on the range, you also could play your round at your home course differently—by hitting tee shots that will leave long-iron approaches. An actual green is a better target for practicing than anything you are likely to find on the practice range.

If at all possible, use a caddie. A friend or family member should more than suffice. This person probably won't do anything more than carry your clubs, unless it's another good golfer who can dispense advice and read putts, but at least the burden of lugging equipment around a golf course will no longer be yours. You want to be physically and mentally fit throughout the round and lightening the load doesn't hurt.

Out on Tour I look for a couple of simple things from my caddie. One, I want him to be on time. As banal as this may sound, you could ask every single tour pro what the single most important aspect of caddying is and to the man they will say showing up on time. Tour players are the best golfers in the world. They know their games. They can hit shots better than anyone and they are the world's best putters. But it all goes for naught if they show up for practice and the caddie is missing or, even worse, they show up for actual play and the caddie and clubs are nowhere to be seen.

That said, I look for a little more than punctuality. I want accurate yardages. My caddie must not only be able to read a yardage book—and the ones we get on Tour are pretty complex—but he must also put in the legwork before the tournament to make sure that the yardage book is accurate.

Then he must know my game, know how far I generally hit each club. I say "generally" because I can hit a 5-iron lots of different yardages. But if I hit a normal 5-iron, say, 185 yards, then the caddie must know it. That's because I can never rule out the situation where club selection may be difficult or awkward. In such situations, I don't want my caddie to pull the club for me, but I do want him to contribute to the decision, and he can do that only if he knows my yardages with each club.

He also should know golf himself. He should be a pretty good player, so he can understand certain situations and, again, be able to contribute to the conversation when I need him to. If I'm having trouble deciding whether to lay up in front of a barranca or try to clear it, he should know why I may want to do each of those things, and anticipate the consequences. He can do that only if he has the mind of a golfer.

And he should be businesslike, for the simple reason that, just as playing golf is my business, so caddieing is *his* business. He should approach it as such.

There have been instances during my career when the caddie has come to my rescue. I'll never forget what happened when I was playing in the British Open at St.

Andrews. The 12th hole at the Old Course is one of the great unknown challenges in the game. It's a short par four on which the landing area for a tee shot hit with a wood is literally pock-marked with pot bunkers. And, as with just about every hole on the Old Course, the fairways seem to channel balls into them. Up ahead, the green is two-tiered with a steep slope separating the two tiers. So if you end up in one of the pots, it's tough enough to hit the green, but hitting the correct tier is all but impossible. There is a narrow stretch of fairway to the right of the bunkers, but that's a risky proposition with a fence and out of bounds off to the right. The only smart play, really, is to lay up off the tee with an iron.

For three days I hit a fairway wood and for three days I got into trouble. On the fourth day, I left the 11th green and walked up to the 12th tee. My caddie wasn't looking at me. He was just staring off down the hole. Then I noticed something—he had covered my woods with a towel! He didn't want to discuss anything, did not want to get involved in any argument. He just knew what the smart play was, and he was right. Finally I parred the hole.

It's also good to have someone to chat with, too, so it helps if your caddie and you share a few similar interests. Hunting, perhaps, or sports. This allows you to relax your mind between shots. The last thing you want is to be walking down the fairway and say "How about those Cardinals?" only for your caddie to reply, "Who are the Cardinals?"

But what happens if the arrangement goes bad? You may inadvertently end up with a caddie who not only dispenses bad advice but doesn't realize he's doing so and never lets up. In such situations, you must take action immediately. If the caddie cannot be replaced, then he must be told in no uncertain terms that his job from here on in is to carry the bag. Now you call on all your other instincts. Read your own yardages, select your own clubs, read your own putts. It's certainly not the ideal way to play, but it's better than the alternative.

Maintaining an even disposition during tournament play is essential, because it is during a tournament, more than any other time, that you are liable to go off the rails. Pressure can make your pulse race, can make your breathing quicken, can make your hands sweat.

There are various ways to deal with this. You can visit with a sports psychologist or read about techniques for keeping a sound mental state—there are plenty of good "mental side" books out there. I do neither, but that's just the way I am. Human beings are all different, and what doesn't work for me may indeed work for you. It's worth a try.

I've found that the best way to stay calm on the course is to think about non-golf things between shots. As I just mentioned, you could think about hunting or sports, and discuss them with your caddie (or even another player). I usually like to think about my family, about upcoming vacations or birthdays, about past vacations or birthdays, about where my wife and I might be eating that evening, about any movies we've been to or are planning to attend. I also like to fish and hunt, and I'll often think about past fishing and hunting trips.

Other players have different techniques. Fuzzy Zoeller

whistles between shots not because he's an inveterate tunesmith but because it keeps his mind off the pressure. Lee Trevino likes to talk. There's that classic exchange from the British Open at Muirfield in 1972 when Tony Jacklin, in the final group with Lee, complained about Lee's constant chatter.

"Lee, I don't want to talk today," Jacklin is reported to have said.

"Tony, you don't have to talk," Lee replied. "You just have to listen."

The one-shot-at-a-time approach really helps your mental state when you play in a stroke-play tournament. I try to eliminate from my mind what anyone else is doing, what the leading scores may be, how the favorites to win may be playing. It's just me against the golf course.

And as far as I can determine, opportunity always lies ahead of you. If something has gone bad in the past, if you failed to make par on what is a relatively easy hole, then you could look on it as an opportunity lost—but it doesn't have any effect on the opportunities that may lie ahead of you. Play each shot as it comes and sooner or later opportunities will come up.

Even then you should not be disappointed if you don't make the most of your opportunities. Let me ask you: How often does a touring professional hole a putt from 10 feet? You probably figure that we can make two of three. Not true. A study done by one of the major sporting magazines several years ago discovered that top players in the world get down in one from ten feet only 54 percent of the time. Now figure that making the most of your opportunities probably is a little tougher than holing a 10-foot putt. You've busted one longer than ever. Now you face the shortest iron you've ever hit to a particular green. Does that mean you should make birdie? No, only that you have a better opportunity than usual. If you don't make it, move on.

I also find it helps my mental state to remember that playing golf is simply a matter of trying to turn fantasy into reality and understanding when that's too much to ask for. In other words, I hope to hit certain shots—that's the fantasy—but the reasonable expectation of executing them as hoped is the reality. In the two-plus decades since I turned pro, I have come to understand that when you try to make reality out of something that is pure fantasy, you are trying to force things to happen. When you do that, usually something does happen—something bad.

A calm mental state also is important in match play; tactics may change, however. Whereas stroke play is a case of you against the golf course for 18 holes per round, match play is about waging a different war each hole. When the hole is done, it is finished. War is over. A new one is about to begin. You do not have to worry about your score—although you do have to worry about the other player. In stroke play if you double bogey a hole you lose two strokes to the field, at least in theory, and will always be two strokes back until either you make up the strokes or the players ahead of you get into trouble; in match play you begin every hole even.

Not that this is always good. Because it's how you *finish* each hole that counts. Low score wins the hole. So even though you start each hole anew, if you've lost the previous one you're still behind.

That's why it's important in a match-play tournament to bear down, focus on and commit to each shot from the first blow. Too many players take it easy early in a match, figuring there's plenty of time to catch up, and that it's better to lose a hole early than lose a hole late. Not really. A touchdown in football counts for six points in the first minute and six points in the last minute. A solo home run in baseball puts a run on the board whether it's hit in the first inning or the last. If you lose the first hole in a match, not only does it count against you to the same degree as it would on the 18th hole, but the fact is that the odds of reaching that 18th hole are slightly longer. It's absolutely key that you go 100 percent from the first shot.

About the only time you should let up in match play is when your opponent has found real trouble on a hole. I don't mean you should be lenient. Rather, figure out what score will safely win the hole. The last thing you want to do is follow your opponent into trouble. In stroke play you want to play each shot individually with the ultimate goal being that you play each hole in the fewest number of shots. In match play you want to play each shot individually, but you also are trying to be a little smarter, because now you have only to play the hole in one fewer shot than your opponent. There's a little more strategy involved.

Let's say you're playing a hole with water in front of the green but a safe area of fairway off to one side. Your opponent hits it in the water. You can reach the green with your approach but it's a high-risk shot because of the water. Your opponent elects to replay the shot, which is one of his options. He hits it in the water again. At this point, making par on the hole ceases to exist as an option for him. You take the water out of play by hitting to the safe area of fairway and trying to get up and down for par. If you don't bogey will win the hole. So a four or a five are the options, and either will win.

Or think of it this way: par does not exist in match play. Only low score does. It doesn't matter if you score 60 or 600. If you get your ball into the hole in fewer strokes more often than your opponent, you'll win the match, and that's all that counts.

Now let me come back to the concept of "four or a five are the options" because it exists in stroke play, too. In the Masters in 1985, Curtis Strange rebounded after a first-round 81 to gain the lead on the back nine Sunday (as good example of the one-shot-at-a-time concept as you will find). On the par-five 13th, the hole which has Rae's Creek running in front of the green, he hit a pretty good drive, then had to decide what club to hit next. His options were to lay up and get on in three, then two-putt for par, or go for the green in two and make four, perhaps three (this assumes, of course, that he wouldn't three-putt—a safe assumption). But going for the green meant that he would have to carry the water with a fairway wood. Much better to carry it with a short iron.

In the broadcast booth, Ken Venturi said that Curtis should lay up, because the most likely number that Curtis would shoot on the hole, and we're talking an almost air-tight prediction, would be a four or a five. But when Curtis pulled out a wood, Ken correctly pointed out that now three, four, five, six and seven all were possible. Of those five numbers, one was preferable, two were identical, and, most important, two were just not the numbers you should entertain on the back nine of a major championship on a Sunday afternoon. And Curtis did make seven, after hitting into the creek and eventually getting on in five. In fairness to Curtis, he can hit a green with a fairway wood quite easily, but this was a case in which on-in-two was a low-percentage shot, a fantasy, and on-in-three was high-percentage, a reality.

It's key no matter the format you're playing that you focus and commit to your shot. We discussed before the importance of having a good and regular pre-shot routine, with a trigger to start the focus. It's equally important that when you focus on your shot, you're thinking only of hitting the shot you've visualized. It definitely is not a good idea to think about the outcome of the shot. You should not be thinking "If I can get this close and make the putt I'll win the hole" or "If I can hit this stiff, I'll grab the lead," because these thoughts will take focus away from the matter at hand, the hitting of the golf ball. In fact, winning tournaments is about nothing more than that: hitting the golf ball better than the other guys.

In tournaments, more than any other time, it's important to stick to your routine. If you are distracted by anything, step away and start again. It could be a thought about where the ball might land. It could be a sudden gust of wind. It could be a shred of doubt creeping into your mind about club selection. It doesn't matter. Step away.

But the ultimate message I want to pass on about playing a tournament is that old Yogi Berra cliché, It's never over 'til it's over.

Okay, 12 strokes back, one hole to play, that is over

(but you could still play the final hole well enough to restore your confidence, find out something about the hole for future use, or just enjoy yourself). But when a few holes are left to play in stroke play, or when *the match is still alive no matter the score* in match play, you must continue to do everything you know you must do in tournament golf, everything you have been practicing and preparing during all those hours on the practice tee and the course. If you cannot get this frame of mind engraved in your brain, you will never be a good tournament golfer.

Look at Jack Nicklaus in the 1986 Masters. With nine holes to play, he was making a move, but in contention that year were Greg Norman, Seve Ballesteros, Tom Kite, Nick Price, Corey Pavin, Bernhard Langer—a truly star-studded leaderboard. And even if it's one thing to be Jack Nicklaus, the man who once birdied his last five holes to win a tournament (1978 Jackie Gleason Inverrary Classic), it's another to assume these other top names would just fall by the wayside.

If you watched this tournament, you know that they didn't. Many of them played very well. Corey Pavin was in the hunt until he hit into water on the par-three 16th. Kite missed a putt that would have tied Jack, and Greg overjuiced his approach to the final green, missing it right and making bogey. But Jack just kept grinding out low scores—there goes that grinding thing again—and returned a 31 on the back nine.

And who would have thought I would be in with a chance of winning the 1991 U.S. Open? I was there on an exemption. With 18 holes to play I was in 21st place. With eight holes to play in the final round, 15 players were ahead of me. But four birdies in a row got me into the top four, and eventually I won.

Go figure.

No, figure this. Golf is a very, very difficult game that requires a lot of practice, a lot of all the things we've talked about so far, and a little luck. But more than anything it requires that you be smart about every facet of the game.

If you can do that, well, anything can happen.

10

Smart Thoughts, Smart Shots......................

I'd like to finish with what I call "smart thoughts" and "smart shots." Some of these will echo what we have discussed in far greater detail in previous chapters, but they also will crystallize the concept of smart golf into bite-sized portions. You may not be able to memorize all of them but, if you can tuck them away in your mind, they may become available at opportune times. Here goes:

- Smart golf is about managing your game *off* the golf course so you can manage it better *on* the golf course.

- Every golfer can play smarter golf simply because no golfer plays 100 percent smart golf.

- Smart golf is about *decreasing* your score in stroke play and *increasing* your ability to win holes in match play.

- Smart golf isn't about technique—even though it's a smart idea to have good technique.

- Smart golf is about doing everything right so that your technique takes care of itself.

- Smart golf is about increasing your expectations realistically—and then meeting those expectations and increasing them again.

- *Quality* of practice time is far more important than quantity.

- Before a round, practice your complete game. After a round, practice what needs work.

- Practice at home whenever (and wherever) possible.

- Study and try as many different components of golf equipment as possible before deciding on what to use.

- Consult a qualified PGA of America professional to determine the proper specifications for your equipment.

- *Never* be reluctant to get a second opinion.

- Keep all your equipment in good condition.

- Keep a checklist of equipment you'll need on the course, and always refer to it before leaving home.

- A golfer in good mental condition always will outplay a golfer who doesn't think properly.

- Always remain confident in your game and your abilities.

- Stay in shape—golf can take more out of you than you think.

- It is important to eat and drink well.

- Always have a game plan going into a round of golf. It could be mental or physical, or both.

- *Always* count your clubs before starting to play.

- In general, hit tee shots *with* the slope of the fairway and approach shots *into* the slope of the green.

- Play every hole backwards in your mind before playing it forward for real.

- A pre-shot routine is vital to playing smart golf because it gets you into the proper state of mind to execute the shot.

- Try to find a trigger to start your pre-shot routine. In between each shot and the trigger, you need not think about your game.

- Remember all the components of a correct decision: the lie, your yardage, the weather conditions, the shape of the shot you want to hit, where you want your ball to finish up. When you have processed all these and have chosen the club, you must commit to the shot absolutely.

- Remember that the better your decisions, the fewer decisions you will have to make.

- If anything interferes with your pre-shot routine, back off and start again.

- No more than two swing thoughts—tempo and one other. Or just go with tempo.

- You will hit many more greens in regulation if you hit fairways in regulation—in one stroke.

- Accuracy, therefore, is the absolute priority of the smart golfer.

- When you definitely cannot hit a green in one shot, figure out the two easiest shots that will get you close.

- If you are between clubs, take the longer one.

- Never assume that you can easily duplicate the best shot you ever hit with a particular club. Think instead of the typical shot with the club.

- Don't try to hit the ball harder when hitting into the wind. Hit easier.

- Similarly, in windy conditions, don't swing harder— swing *better*.

- Although you always should have a target in mind with every shot, the target should become more precise the closer you get to the hole.

- Always get out of trouble as quickly as possible by hitting the easiest recovery.

- Don't try to make up a lost stroke by hitting an impossible shot.

- On every short-game shot, aim for a specific target in the shape of an imaginary target.

- Study the possible landing areas for short shots before hitting.

- Try to hole every chip.

- Always try to putt from below the hole.

- When reading break in a green, err by reading "too much" break. That way, if you miss, you'll miss on the pro side—the side above the hole. A ball that is missing below the hole will not roll uphill, but a ball that is missing above it might roll in.

- A ball that is not hit hard enough to reach the hole will not go in the hole—obvious, perhaps, but too often forgotten.

- Always study what a missed putt does after it passes the hole.

- If there is any chance at all that your putt may strike an opponent's ball mark, ask him to move it.

- If you have to move your ball mark, remember to put it back in its original position before replacing your ball.

- Never hit tap-ins nonchalantly. You may even miss the ball.

- Remember: A one-inch putt counts the same on the scorecard as a 250-yard drive.

- Never pay attention to what an opponent or fellow competitor is doing. It is out of your control.

- Always play your own game; don't try for added distance because your opponent is long, or try to hit shots to impress another player.

- Always play at your own pace—except if you are in danger of delaying play and earning a penalty.

- Be ready to play when it is your turn. Never waste time—you have a responsibility to other golfers.

- Don't play defensively—if you play not to lose you tend not to win.

- Finish each match with a handshake and a kind word for the other players.

- Always pay your bets promptly—when you start playing smarter golf you will want your beaten opponents to return the favor.

- And remember—*to some, golf is a living; to all of us, it is a game.*

Index.....................................